CAPITAL COPS

The Unofficial Guide to Delhi Police

CAPITAL COPS

The Unofficial Guide to Delhi Police

Suvashis Choudhary

HAR-ANAND
PUBLICATIONS PVT LTD

Published by Ashok Gosain and Ashish Gosain for:
HAR-ANAND PUBLICATIONS PVT LTD
E-49/3, Okhla Industrial Area, Phase-II, New Delhi-110020
Tel: 41603490
E-mail: info@haranandbooks.com/haranand@rediffmail.com
Shop online at: www.haranandbooks.com

Printed in India

To every capital cop
who joins, serves and
departs in anonymity.

Contents

Foreword

Flipping the pages of this well written book on Delhi Police was, for me, going down the memory lane. A memory, very fond to my heart, of leading the fabulous force called Delhi Police. I felt, as before, of visiting a police station for the customary inspection, walking the lanes of Old Delhi to oversee police bandobast during a festival, getting a briefing on the investigation at a crime scene or walking down the Rajpath on the eve of Republic day arrangements.

In the early eighties Delhi Police had successfully organised the Asian Games and the Commonwealth Heads of Govt Meet. But subsequently for most part of the decade, it had been fighting a completely new battle, terrorism. It was in the midst of this that I took over as Commissioner of Delhi Police in 1988. This was the time when the author, Suvashis also joined Delhi Police after completing his training. He was posted at the sensitive Chanakyapuri subdivision, which not only comprised important locations of the capital city including Rashtrapati Bhawan and Prime Minister's residence but was the focal point of public demonstrations and agitations, which are an important part of democracy. He handled the responsibility with a maturity far beyond his age. The same maturity is evident now in the book and in the manner in which he has tried to unclutter the working of the police organisation without trying to cover the warts or to find excuses for them.

For most of the citizens of Delhi, a Police station remains an enigma. The author has in a very easy-to-understand way unravelled this important institution and showed that far from being a monolithic black box it is a place where citizen's complaints are received, processed and taken to a logical conclusion, in a dynamic interplay of several sub-systems. In doing this, he has also explained the process of criminal investigation in a very interesting way. Chapter after chapter, he lays bare the structure and functioning of various units of Delhi Police in a manner which can be easily comprehended by the common citizen. If for nothing else, I recommend this book to all citizens to keep as a ready reckoner for all things Police. Moreover, I encourage the younger generation of Police officers to use this book to imbibe the heritage and ethos of their ever-evolving department.

After having read the book, I realized with great satisfaction that the initiatives we undertook for police-public cooperation in Delhi are being taken forward by the later generations of police officers. We started many programmes to ensure participation of the citizens in policing and ensured that citizens become aware of their rights and duties with regard to police. But most importantly, we had to change the behaviour of the police when dealing with the people. I depended a lot on the young ACPs and DCPs to carry forward this message to the rank and file of Delhi Police and implement the new policing culture in its true spirit. Young officers like the author, fresh out of university and with idealism in their hearts, became my comrade in arms. Going through the book, I could feel the fervour of the old times and also got a glimpse of how the process had unfolded and how it was perceived by the stake-holders. The recent events in which Delhi Police has been in the limelight, underscores the importance of taking the people along in ushering a crime free and safe city. As a Police chief then, and as a commoner now, I know enough to reassure all citizens that Delhi Police is, with you, for you, always.

Raja Vijay Karan
Former Commissioner of Police, Delhi

Chapter 1

Introduction

The word 'Police' the world over evokes myriad emotions, varying from fear to loathing, from indignation to indifference. Very rarely is it appreciation or adulation. This extreme swing is attributed to the peculiar position of the police in the arrangement of societal institutions. The police is invariably juxtaposed between the citizen and what he considers and believes to be his inalienable right.

We'll begin with a story about a peace-loving citizen whose house was burgled while he was at work and his family away on vacation. He went to the police who very reluctantly and after much dilly-dallying registered his complaint. Already tormented with the loss he had suffered, the attitude of the police annoyed him further. While driving back home he got a call from his wife and he started updating her on the unfortunate developments. Just then the traffic police pulled him over. He tried to explain his situation, but the officers were in no mood to let him go unless he paid a traffic fine of Rs. 1000. Then they made an alternative offer. Pay up Rs. 500 as bribe to escape the fine. He paid the amount and was satisfied on having saved some money. Just then he received a call from the police informing him of catching a person under suspicious circumstances with a lorry full of household articles, which they wanted him to identify. He marvelled at their alertness and rushed to the police station. The police was very helpful and the man was relieved to find all his stolen belongings. He learned that the burglar's accomplice had managed to escape with all the stolen cash. For several days, he pursued and persuaded the police to make a serious effort to arrest the accomplice and recover his money. The police, however, had other important cases to handle and, therefore, did not give as much priority to his case. When the absconder was finally caught, there was no cash left as he had spent it all. The law-abiding person was aggrieved. He felt that the police are only good enough to harass citizens like him for minor issues like a traffic offence but were unable to recover his large amount of stolen cash.

This imaginary citizen's experience illustrates the myriad ways in which police can bring either joy or sorrow in a person's life. Let's now move on from the hypothetical anecdote to a real-life incident, which the readers will easily identify with. I am referring to the Nirbhaya episode. In the closing days of 2012, a young student in Delhi was brutally raped in a moving bus by six males, which included a minor. Her male companion was also severely beaten up and both were dumped on the road to die. The incident was so gruesome that it shocked the conscience of the entire nation. Huge protests erupted all over the country. In New Delhi, the protestors repeatedly clashed with the police demanding the sacking of the Police Commissioner. The entire city came to a standstill. Meanwhile, the police conducted a speedy investigation of this blind case and within a week, they had not only identified the suspects but also arrested them from different parts of the country. The case was also sent to court for trial after the conclusion of investigation, within a very short time, not seen very often. The quality of investigation was so good that recently even the country's highest court lauded the police for investigating the case in a fool proof manner and in such a short time.

Nevertheless, at that time, the people were in no mood to listen and the agitation continued with a lot of mayhem and damage on both sides. It also spread a sense of insecurity among the people of Delhi. 'Isn't it the responsibility of the police to prevent such incidents?' people asked. 'How can the police prevent such a crime which is the product of a sick mind nurtured in a life of filth, poverty and deprivation; societal problems, we are not responsible for?' 'It is not possible to provide individual protection to citizens and we did what we could, to catch the perpetrators,' the police said. Although the police chief survived, the episode left many bruised feelings in its trail. The police tried to minimize the damage by reaching out to citizens. However, the nagging question remains: Could the bitter after-taste of this police-citizen face off have been avoided?

Delhi Crime' a Netflix show is set in the aftermath of the heinous 2012 gang rape case that made headlines all over and cemented the city's reputation as the 'Rape Capital of the World'. But it is told from the unlikely perspective of the police - which is botherfreshing and problematic.

The Delhi Police, like most law enforcement organisations around the world, is burdened by a reputation as complicated as that of the city it serves to protect. Alot was written about its handling of the case - it was praised for having nabbed the culprits in a matter of days and filing a detailed chargesheet that was instrumental in their sentencing, but it was also questioned about its ability to prevent such crimes, and criticised for letting redtape get in the way of the investigation.

(Rohan Naahar's review of the Netflix show Delhi Crime in HindustanTimes, 20 April 2019.)

Sceptics among the police feel that do whatever they might, the citizens will always have a negative opinion of them. They go on to assert, something very surprising. 'You won't get a positive feedback from the people unless you do something illegal to help them. You use third degree methods to recover a person's stolen cash and he'll praise you: otherwise, he becomes a vocal critic. You let off a traffic offender after taking a bribe and he's happy.' They further complain that people do not come forward to share information about crimes and criminals and even if they do, they refuse to testify as witnesses in court, a mandatory requirement of criminal procedure. This unhelpful attitude encourages crime and criminals. The citizens, on the other hand, feel that the police are unresponsive to the needs of the common citizens. They are hand in glove with the criminals. Once you grease their palms, they can even bend the rules. 'Show me the face and I will show you the rule' is an oft-repeated mantra used to describe the working principle of the police force.

In that sense, Delhi Police is typical of any police force in the world. Its image and perception undergo an ebb and flow with the vicissitude of people's expectations. The negative image projected in the media does not help either. While many of the expectations people have of the police are reasonable and legitimate, there are others that the police simply cannot fulfil.

Is it then possible to have a meeting ground where there is mutual appreciation of the roles, limitations and expectations? Is it possible to define the boundaries of accepted behaviour? This will be possible only when citizens are aware of the inner working of the police organization with all its strengths and weaknesses. Only then would they be able to evaluate the functioning of the police and analyze media reports of the police's failures and successes in a dispassionate and objective way. A population aware of its rights would be less fearful and, therefore, less vulnerable to extortion and harassment by unscrupulous police officers. The police will also gain by this transparency. The operating environment of the police would improve considerably, once the rules of the game are laid on the table.

There would be less frustration on non-fulfilment of expectations and therefore fewer complaints against the police. The honest and sincere officers would be reassured that the public is not painting every police officer with the same brush. Most importantly, there would be proper benchmarking of police-practices for recalibration of internal processes in the police department. Therefore, there is considerable need to unravel the working of the police for the sake of informed debate in society.

Look at it in another way. Is it not ironical that citizens, the recipients of police service live in fear of the police, which exists solely for eliminating their fear? Is it not desirable to achieve a state where law-abiding citizens have full faith in the law enforcement machinery? A public service institution that touches the lives of people in so many different ways cannot afford to operate in an environment of ignorance and mutual distrust.

This book aims to eliminate this lack of awareness by demystifying the police organization so that the citizens and scholars, writing on police, have a fair idea of their strengths and vulnerabilities. In order to do this, it is important to understand the organization, its processes and its inner functioning. Knowledge of Delhi Police would prove helpful in knowing about other police forces in India, as the organization and systems as well as the broad statutes governing the police are similar.

DELHI POLICE

Like any other police force in India, Delhi Police is a law enforcement agency, an important organ of the criminal justice system. Law and order is a state subject, implying that it is the prerogative of states to have administrative and operational control over the police, provided it is operated under the Constitution of India and the various laws prevailing at the time. In the case of Delhi Police, however, there is one major departure. Since it is entrusted with the task of policing the national capital, it is not under the control and superintendence of Delhi's State government but is directly controlled by the Central Government through the Lieutenant Governor (LG).

From Kotwal, during the Delhi Sultanate to Police Commissioner in the present era, Delhi Police has come a long way. The earliest recorded police officer called the Kotwal was appointed during the reign of Alauddin Khilji (1296-1316). Later, in 1648 with the shifting of the Mughal capital from Agra to Delhi, a Kotwal was appointed to oversee the administration of Shahjahanabad, as Delhi was then called. The Kotwal sitting at the police station called Kotwali was the main officer entrusted with the administration of the city and this arrangement continued till the arrival of the British in Delhi in the early nineteenth century. At the time of the First war of Indian Independence of 1857, there were several other police stations besides Kotwali, namely Paharganj, Badarpur, Alipur and a police post at Yamuna Bridge. During those tumultuous days, Police Station Kotwali, situated at Chandni Chowk, was a nerve centre of activities. In the immediate aftermath of the rebellion, it was a scene of executions of the rebels.

The modern police force that we know today was set up under the Police Act of 1861. Five police stations, viz. Subzi Mandi, Nangloi, Mehrauli, Sadar Bazar and Kotwali, were created in the same year. The first ever First Information Report (FIR) was registered in PS Subzi Mandi on 18 October

1861, which, perhaps, marks the beginning of the modern criminal justice system in Delhi. In the intervening century and a half, Delhi Police was witness to small and big upheavals, each of which had the potential to change the destiny of the entire nation. Right from the transfer of the Imperial capital from Calcutta (now Kolkata) to Delhi, the struggle for independence (culminating in the 'tryst of destiny' on 15 August 1947), the partition riots and influx of refugees, the assassination of Mahatma Gandhi, the challenges of nation-building in the initial years, the Emergency, assassination of the former prime minister, Indira Gandhi, the anti-Sikh riots to terrorism of different hues, there are several incidents that stand out from a long list of momentous events in the history of India. Delhi Police has gone through it all, learning, forgetting and relearning important lessons which history was hell-bent on teaching it.

The identity of the contemporary Delhi Police is a product of this accumulated experience of the last century and a half. Initially created as a part of Punjab Police, it got its first Inspector General of Police (IGP) on 16 February 1948 now celebrated every year as its Raising Day. From a very diminutive size, Delhi Police grew in leaps and bounds trying to keep pace with the city's bourgeoning population and escalating problems. Today, it comprises 163 territorial police stations with a total strength of nearly 87,000 police officers of different ranks. Although the number is still inadequate for the growing population of the city, it has a dominant presence in terms of the 1500 sq. km area that it is mandated to police.

The origin of the police organization in its complexity, as seen today, can be traced to the humble beginnings of a police station in the early days. In its most basic form, the police station was performing several functions including investigation of crime, crowd management, traffic control, intelligence collection and myriad other law enforcement duties. It was a kind of pastoral setting and the simplicity was reflected in the pattern of crime and law enforcement challenges. With increasing population, urbanization and concomitant socio-economic changes, the roles and responsibilities of the police station became increasingly diverse. To keep up with the changing times and demands, various functions started getting hived off from the police station and were assigned to specialized units. As a part of this evolutionary process, the Special Branch was created for intelligence collection, Crime Branch for investigation of special types of crime, Traffic Police for traffic control and Armed Police for law and order duties. Police Control Room (PCR) was set up with wireless-equipped cars to act as the first responder to distress calls made by the public on a Police Dial 100 facility. Over the years, several other units were added to the organization as per the emerging needs of policing an increasingly complex society. A Special Cell was constituted for terrorism-related crimes, Economic Offences Wing (EOW) for economic offences like cheating and forgery, Cyber Crime Cell (now, CyPAD) for cyber offences and a Special Police Unit for Women and Children (SPUWAC) was later formed for crimes against women and children. Some of the existing conventional entities like Recruitment and Training, Vigilance and Communication units expanded in scale and complexity. Since all the units had to work under one umbrella organization of Delhi Police, there was a need for control and coordination which gave rise to a strong Police Headquarter (PHQ) populated by several supervisory levels. The Delhi Police that we see today is the outcome of this organic process of differentiation and specialization.

Despite the structural and functional diversity of the police organization, its core functions, namely prevention and investigation of conventional crime as well as law enforcement, remain with the police station. The fundamental reason is that it is the legally designated place where a citizen can lodge an FIR regarding the commission of a crime. The investigation of the case begins only with the registration of the FIR and concludes with the filing of the Final Report in a court of law. After that, a trial is conducted in the court culminating in the final judgement. This can then be appealed in successively higher courts up to the Supreme Court of India. The entire judicial process is independent of the police.

The powers to register an FIR, investigate cases, arrest the accused, search and seize property as well as several other powers of the police including 'use of force' are drawn from various laws passed by the legislature. Laws also prescribe rules. These rules lay down the details for implementing the laws. The earliest law under which police was created and which gave them powers was the Indian Police Act 1861. There are two broad categories of laws in India that concern the police. The major acts, namely the Indian Penal Code (IPC) of 1860 defines the offences with penal provisions and the Criminal Procedure Code (CrPC) of 1973 lays down the procedures to be followed by the criminal justice system. The Evidence Act of 1872, concerns evidence to be used during the trial.

Apart from the major acts, there are numerous Special Laws, which are specific laws for special types of crime like Arms Act, Gambling Act, NDPS Act, Dowry Act, and so on. There are also local laws applicable in certain geographical areas like the Delhi Police Act, 1978.

Cases are registered under one, or several, sections of law from the IPC or any special law. For example, if a murder has been committed by using a weapon the FIR would mention the sections of law, namely 302 IPC read with Section 27 of the Arms Act. The trial court would charge the accused under these sections. All the procedures undertaken during investigation and trial will be strictly as per CrPC. A person, whether he is a complainant, a witness or an accused has certain rights, which are supposed to be respected by the police. The principles of human rights are also to be strictly followed by the law enforcement agencies and in the event of a violation, the aggrieved party can move the court.

One important local act is the Delhi Police Act of 1978, which ushered in the Police Commissionerate system in Delhi. It was a much-needed legislation to change the police system in keeping with the changing requirements of law enforcement for a growing capital city. Contemporary Delhi Police draws its mandate and powers from this Act. One important legacy of Delhi being part of Greater Punjab Province was the Punjab Police Rules 1934 called the PPR. The three-volume PPR was an exhaustive and detailed set of rules for guiding the structure and function of police in the erstwhile state of Punjab. The PPR is still prevalent in Haryana, Himachal Pradesh and Punjab, besides Delhi, all of which were in the erstwhile state of Punjab. The police force in the Punjab province of Pakistan also follows the PPR till date, despite the partition of the province in 1947. This is not to say that the police are trapped in a time warp unaffected by the developments of the intervening years, including the country's Independence and Partition. To the contrary, it speaks volumes for the timeless nature of the well-drafted PPR. Undoubtedly, the police organization has undergone a sea change but the core functions of law enforcement like detection and investigation of crime remain the same.

The relationship of police and the citizens is both symbiotic and synergistic. However, this special relationship can be nurtured for creating an orderly society by making the population aware of its rights as well as responsibilities in relation to police. Rights provided to citizens as complainants, as suspects, as accused, as witnesses, and as recipients of police service should be protected in full measure. Similarly, citizens should show responsibility with regard to assisting the police in its law enforcement functions by providing information about crimes and criminals, by ensuring peace and order in their sphere of influence and by being responsible citizens. The sooner both police and the citizens of Delhi recognize that their destiny is inextricably intertwined, the better it would be for the city.

CHAPTER 2

Flesh and Blood

The Men Who Matter

To say, Delhi Police is a microcosm of the society it is mandated to serve, is not just a manner of introducing a new chapter. This is an apt description of a police force under the control of the Union Government with its officers drawn from all over the country. The only reason it is not an identical replica of India's diversity is the preference of people to work closer to their native place and the prohibitive distance to Delhi. Even so, senior officers of the force are pan India as are the middle level officers. However, the lower rungs of police are predominantly from the hinterlands of Delhi. It is not easy to become a member of Delhi Police, even at the constabulary level, given its popularity in the neighbouring states.

At nine every morning, when most of Delhi citizens are on the road rushing to work, they are likely to find some khaki-clad persons with DP emblazoned silver badge on their shoulders rushing to catch a bus or the metro. Most of their colleagues, especially those in 'field postings', would already be at work, at traffic junctions, in PCR vans or stepping out of police stations after their morning briefing by the SHO. Similarly, on weekends and holidays when most people either relax or have an outing with their families, policemen and policewomen are out with the same earnestness. 'We see our children grow up horizontally,' they joke, implying that they find their children sleeping when they leave home in the early hours and again find them in bed, when they return late in the night.

It is also true that some never return to their families ever, consumed either by the lawlessness of the street or by the inherent risks in their jobs. What is also unfortunate is that some policemen succumb to their own inability to handle stress. But most do not seem to complain having accepted the tough requirements of their chosen vocation. They are aware that it is not easy to adapt to this tough life, but neither is it easy to join this force.

THE GAZETTED OFFICERS (GOs)

Delhi Police is a hierarchical organisation with the Commissioner of Police at the top, and the Constable at the bottom of the rung. Any young man or woman with a desire to enter the police force can do so at three levels depending upon their educational qualification, and of course, age. These are, at the level of Gazetted Officers (GOs), the Sub Inspectors (SIs) and Constables. The highest level is the Indian Police Service (IPS), the members of which are allotted the AGMUT Cadre, which stands for Arunachal, Goa, Mizoram and Union Territory. (With the inclusion of Jammu & Kashmir and Ladakh as Union Territories, these two UTs have also been included in the same cadre for all-India services). The other service is DANIPS, its full form being Delhi and Andaman and Nicobar Islands Police Service. The nomenclature of this central service is not apt since the members of this cadre are posted in Delhi as well as other Union Territories, namely Chandigarh, Daman and Diu, Dadra and Nagar Haveli, Andaman and Nicobar Islands and Lakshadweep except the UT of Puducherry. Both these services — IPS and DANIPS —

are recruited from among the candidates who pass the Civil Services Examination conducted every year by the Union Public Service Commission. However, candidates who are higher up in that examination in the merit list are allotted IPS. Although both IPS and DANIPS officers start at the level of the Assistant Commissioner of Police (ACP), the former get promoted faster. DANIPS officers also get promoted to the IPS cadre but after a time lag, depending on several factors including vacancies in the force. The IPS officers along with DANIPS officers are categorized as Gazetted officers (GOs). GOs start at the middle level as an ACP and if one is lucky and young enough at the time of recruitment, he or she can end up as the Commissioner of Police (CP). He passes through years of penance as Assistant Commissioner of Police (ACP), Additional Deputy Commissioner of Police (Addl. DCP), Deputy Commissioner of Police (DCP), Additional CP, Joint CP, Special CP — successively reaching the rarefied environs of police administration. They are the supervisory level officers, and they go on to become policy makers for the force. But things may not be as smooth as they seem since the vagaries of the system, of which there are plenty of examples, may take a toll on their career, their morale or, at worst, their health. One who loses heart falls by the wayside and is soon forgotten.

THE UPPER SUBORDINATES

The cutting-edge level in the organization is the tier below the Gazetted officers—the so-called Upper Subordinates, which is the common category for three hierarchical ranks, starting with the Inspector of Police, the Sub- Inspector (SI) and the Assistant Sub-Inspector (ASI). Police work involves a lot of paperwork and a working knowledge of law. This is done mainly by the cadre of ASIs and SIs. These ranks perform the important function of case investigation and of conducting enquiries. Mostly, their roles are mandated by law and their reports are submitted to a court of law. For example, many investigations can only be conducted by an SI rank, and some functions like seeking police remand of any accused person can be done by an officer not below the ASI rank. The most important function of a police station is investigation of criminal cases and this is largely entrusted to upper subordinates.

Late ACP Virender Singh was recruited as an ASI in Delhi Police. He had countless stories to narrate about his experience as a directly recruited officer at a time when there were very few officers in the force. One comical anecdote was how during a meeting of villagers, seeing his one star and red/blue ribbon on his shoulder, he was taken to be the boss even as his amused SP looked on. They were urging him to scold the SP, who they thought was a constable, for not being seen in the village often.

As ACP of Darya ganj he was the author's mentor during field training in Central district.

From the time a complainant enters the police station, he meets the Duty officer at the front office who records his complaint and assigns it to another officer called the Emergency officer. He is invariably the officer handling the matter and if it is converted to a First Information Report (FIR), he is the designated officer for the Investigation of the case (IO). The officer is associated with the case till the conclusion of investigation and if required, trial in a court. Even if the officer is transferred out of this police station, he remains associated with the case as the first IO. There may be other ranks assisting the IO, but the case gets investigated under his name and he has an important legal status which cannot be delegated to any other rank. All the cases after the finalization of investigation can only be sent to the court by the officer-in-charge of the police station, who is none other than an upper subordinate. In law and order duties also, a SI and an ASI have an important leadership role. They lead their men and are responsible for their actions. They also have to take important decisions like use of force and arrest of offenders. If there is any commission of crime in their presence, the officer has to take preventive action and take up investigation of the case.

In units other than the police station, the SI or the ASI has an important role to perform. For example, an officer of SI or ASI rank is present in the PCR van and is the first responder in any incident where the police receive a call through the control room on Dial 100 facility. In the Traffic Police, an ASI or SI is designated the Zonal Officer (ZO) and is legally empowered to prosecute traffic offenders. In this function he may be assisted by lower subordinates, but he is solely responsible for any legal action taken by him which he has to defend in court. In Special Branch this officer is deputed for intelligence collection which is a crucial input for police decision-making on sensitive issues. In all the functions whether in the police station or any other unit, the ASI and the SI rank is the interface with the public for which common sense, tact and patience are very important attributes.

There is no longer recruitment directly to the post of the ASI as it used to happen till the 1960s. Now they are promoted from among the Head Constables. They graduate to the next higher rank of SI and, age permitting, to the Inspector rank. In the early days, police stations were headed by an SI or an ASI, depending on the importance of the station. But nowadays in Delhi Police, only Inspectors head the police station as the SHO. Though it differs from state to state, in Delhi there is direct entry to the SI level. Although the SI does not enter the force at the rank of a GO, he can very well break into it, albeit at a later stage of his career. But the SI is the main entry route to become an Inspector, a rank from which SHOs are picked.

The Station House Officer (SHO) is the most important functionary in the police organisation when it was originally constituted under the Police Act of 1861, and it still remains so.

> *Late Ranbir Singh was the quintessential SHO of Delhi Police. Very hands-on, he was aware of all the activities of his subordinates and about the activities in his ilaqa. He could sense any problem from before-hand and used to shepherd his staff to take corrective measures. He served under the author more than once. A visit to his PS for inspection was a treat as well as tiresome as he would ensure that his superior officers should see all his good work and initiatives.*

If there is one rank of the police hierarchy which is most well-known to the citizens, it is the SHO. In old vernacular he was called the 'Daroga'. His popularity is linked with the entity he presides over—the police station which is looked at, both in fear and awe, by the common citizen. Various attempts to change his image in Independent India have not borne fruit. It may well be true that both the incumbents and the citizens do not want it to change- the former for reasons of the status quo and the latter for continuing to need an institution which represents and often unleashes raw power. More of it later, when readers will be acquainted with the functioning of the police station which the SHO heads.

THE LOWER SUBORDINATES

Constables and Head Constables together fall in the category of lower subordinates. As on date, constables comprise nearly sixty-five percent of the total strength of Delhi Police. Functionally, they are a very important rank deployed for operations of all sorts. Their generic function can be divided into three parts: core, essential and support. Core duty is the basic function of a constable, like working in the beat of every Police Station, regulating traffic on the roads as traffic constables and performing law and order *bandobast* duties as part of the armed police unit. In present day Delhi, a thriving metropolis with a huge population, the core duties of a constable are numerous. The fact that it is also the seat of the National, State and the Municipal authorities, Delhi Police have to handle numerous law and order arrangements. They also carry out some essential functions like protecting assets, office assistance, assisting core functions and several other duties like in Record Room, Malkhana, guard and lock-up duties and in escorting arrested persons to the court. They also have a support role where they assist the officers in investigation and in other specialized duties in districts and units. Their most basic responsibility, however, is in the Police Station where they are used as beat officers, in law and order duties, in security arrangements and in traffic control. Similarly, there are various other units like Crime Branch, Special Cell and EOW where they are deployed for assisting the IOs with investigation by performing sundry duties like guarding lock-ups and establishments, serving summons, delivering documents and materials to courts and forensic labs etc. In other words, constables being at the bottom of the hierarchical organization perform very important functions. In that role they are at the cutting edge level where they are the first point of contact for the citizens.

This last tier in the police hierarchy is, for me, the most important in Delhi Police, since they are not only the boots on the ground but also determine the culture of the force. They are largest in number and therefore the most visible. Needless to say, the image of police is determined by the behaviour and performance of this important rank. Any effort to change the image of police in the eyes of the public would have to begin at this stratum.

It is not easy to get selected as a police constable in terms of the sheer number of applicants. In the recruitment conducted in 2013, for *each* of the 523 posts of constable there were 455 applications. The job of a constable in Delhi Police remains highly coveted specially for areas around Delhi, like Uttar Pradesh, Haryana and Rajasthan. Lately, there has been an initiative to recruit from other far-flung areas of the country in order to give a more regional representation to this force. The recruitment of a Constable is one of the toughest, more in competition than in content, with a large number of candidates competing for relatively fewer jobs. Moreover, it involves very exacting physical standards, of both endurance and physical measures like the applicant's height and chest. It is, however, ironical that the promotion avenues for this level are very restricted—with only a few passing an exam and physical fitness test to go to the next level of Head Constable (HC)—while the rest stagnating for years before getting promoted—may be only five years before retirement. Some Constables of the former category, who manage to pass the HC examination, can aspire to get promoted to ASI and subsequently to SI before bowing out of service.

After getting promoted to the post of Head Constable, they are supposed to lead the constables on the ground and are responsible for their conduct and behaviour while on duty. The officers and men of Delhi Police are performing a very risky and arduous task that too, at the cost of family time and personal comfort. They deserve some prospects of better promotion even if there are no financial benefits. Since it is a uniformed service, the self-esteem of the men depends on the badge he carries on his shoulder. Apart from the inherent hazards of the job, the constant monitoring by various agencies and the hawk-eye of the media make the work environment of Delhi Police personnel very challenging. The fact that presently nearly a thousand personnel of different ranks are facing departmental proceedings for allegations ranging from corruption, harassment, to high-handedness, speaks about the emphasis on probity in the force. There is no justification for any wrong-doing by any government functionary and it is natural that police force entrusted with law enforcement in the capital of the country has to observe a high standard of professionalism and discipline. But it is imperative that the basic needs of the force like housing, emoluments and promotions are taken care of. However, lately there has been a serious endeavour to remove this anomaly by incorporating a time bound promotion scheme. From the year 2016, the department has started giving *in situ* promotion to constables, HCs and ASIs based on length of service on officiating capacity in order to address this problem of stagnation.

Chapter 3

Hit the Ground Running

Recruitment and Training

Recruitment and training pose a very big challenge for the police organization. To attract the right candidates and to train them for police service in a way that the personnel acquire the necessary knowledge, skill and attitude and fulfil the expectations of the people is not an easy task. Since the police force recruits its personnel at different levels, the recruitment and training processes should reflect the expectations of the community from each of the levels.

Under the Constitution of India, 'Police' is a State subject which gives all the powers to the States under the Union to recruit, train, deploy and utilize the police force as per their need and priority. Recruitment takes place for various ranks as per the Recruitment Rules laid down by different States for their police force. Although Delhi is a State, as mentioned earlier, the powers over the police are vested with the Central Government, which is exercised through the LG. Leaving aside gazetted officers, meaning Assistant Commissioners and above, including the IPS officers at the top, the other ranks, namely, Sub-Inspectors and Constables in Delhi Police are recruited by the organization under the Delhi Police Act 1978 and the various rules framed under the Act. Besides the Act and Rules made by the Government, there are Standing Orders issued by the department to act as a guide for the process of recruitment of these ranks. What makes the process challenging is the requirement of certain physical standards for the recruit in addition to the scholastic requirement and medical fitness.

In India, generally, the recruitment process of a police officer comprises three stages. The first is the test of physical fitness that essentially includes a physical measurement standard and a test of physical endurance (together, called PEMT). Physical measurement is that of height and chest, which depends on the specific requirement of the State. Physical endurance test includes running, long and high jumps and may include some other events as per the requirement. The second stage is the written test comprising various subjects depending on the level of officer being recruited. The last stage is a medical examination of the recruits. However, the physical measurement and endurance test is not done in the case of IPS & Gazetted officers like ACPs, provided they qualify certain minimum benchmark of physical standards laid down in the Civil Services Recruitment Rules. This is tested during the medical examination of selected candidates.

RECRUITMENT PROCESS OF CONSTABLES

In Delhi Police, both males and females are recruited at the level of constable. They do similar work and enjoy equal pay and allowances. At present, educational qualification for recruitment as a constable is 10+2 (senior secondary) and the age limit is 18 to 21. The vast pool of just-out-of-school boys and girls looking for good opportunities for employment and growth, makes the recruitment process for constables in the police and the paramilitary forces a huge logistical challenge. In Delhi Police, in the last 5 years, approximately 6 lakh candidates underwent the physical test of which approximately

2.5 lakh candidates appeared for the written examination competing for 6085 posts.

In the past there have been reports of stampedes or riots during the physical recruitment drives in various parts of the country and often young lives are lost. This happens because of a lack of proper planning in organizing such drives as also the fact that the recruitment system just collapses under the weight of the overwhelming numbers turning up. The problem of handling such a huge number of candidates for recruitment is nowhere more evident than in Delhi. However, Delhi Police are aware of this and extra precautions with meticulous planning are taken at recruitment drives to avoid such eventualities.

The other challenge is to ensure the integrity of the recruitment process. Not only should the entire process remain transparent and fair but the candidates and the general public should also perceive it to be so. To select the right person for the service in terms of skill, knowledge and attitude is the very obvious intention that is true for any organization. It is also obvious that a person who enters any police organization by paying bribes cannot deliver proper service to the community for which he has been recruited. What is not so obvious is the fact that the integrity of the entire organization depends on the credibility of the police recruitment process. Any doubts on this can dent the citizen's perception of the force itself.

This is a very important aspect, the significance of which is often not fully comprehended and therefore needs elaboration. The perception of the quality of service delivered by the police is dependent on the image of how fair and competent the police are seen by the citizens. If rightly or wrongly citizens view the recruitment process as not fair and above board, this factor goes into their evaluation of police service delivery. They will hold the police in very low esteem and the credibility of the force itself would be eroded. And this has a bearing on how safe and secure the citizens feel in the City or State. This is because the feeling of safety and security is primarily psychological. The evaluation process goes beyond statistics and figures. However appetizing food may be in a restaurant, if the cooking process is not perceived to be hygienic the restaurant cannot run for long.

Lately, most police forces in the country are putting a lot of emphasis on making the recruitment process transparent and fair. The Bureau of Police Research and Development (BPR&D), which is under the Ministry of Home Affairs (MHA), has formulated a comprehensive Transparent Recruitment Process (TRP) which several states, including Delhi, have adopted.

TRANSPARENT RECRUITMENT PROCESS (TRP)

A candidate intending to join Delhi Police as a constable has to go through a three-stage elimination process: a Physical Endurance and Measurement Test (PEMT), a Written Test, and a Medical Examination. PEMT is just qualifying in nature and to be able to appear for the written test, every candidate has to clear PEMT. The PEMT consists of three physical endurance tests and two measurements. The physical endurance part consists of running, long jump and high jump, in that order. Only the qualified candidates at every stage go to the next successive stages. After they clear the ground tests, their physical measurement is taken. This consists of measurement of height and chest. The candidates who clear the laid down bench-mark for each event of PEMT individually are declared qualified. The qualified candidates are issued admit cards for the written test which is held only after the PEMT is complete for all who have applied for the post.

The biometric detail of all the PEMT qualified candidates is taken so that there is no impersonation during the next round, viz. the written examination. Apart from biometrics, there is an elaborate system of CCTVs installed to monitor and record the process at each stage of PEMT and the written test. An officer constantly monitors the process from the control room and if he finds any aberration, say for example, a candidate is inadvertently given more than three chances at the high jump event, the supervisor of the event is immediately informed of the lapse. Also, if there is a receipt of a complaint from a candidate at any stage, the recording is replayed and the error rectified. The idea is to make the entire process as foolproof and transparent as possible. This is no small task given the fact that the PEMT is held for about 5-7.5 lakh candidates in each round of recruitment. In the PEMT stage, there are several boards for conducting the test, each headed by a DCP with scores of staff assisting him. Even if each board tests at least 2000 candidates every day, which is a very large number, the number of days works out to be 50 to 60. This is the scale of operation which Delhi Police has to conduct for recruitment of constables ensuring all along, the necessity to keep the process transparent for the entire duration.

The vision of the Project TRP is to ensure a fair, impartial, transparent, objective, tamperproof, scientific, merit-based recruitment process so as to induct into the police, individuals, best suited for their job, who have earned their way into the police on their own merit and without favour or unfair means by using simple but well-defined procedures reinforced by technology and the use of information technology. This vision translates into the ultimate dual goal of improving police image and also raising a force built on foundations of integrity and impartiality.
(Retrieved from www.bprd.nic.in)

Before entry into the venue at the written test, biometric verification of each candidate is done. The written test is still a manual test where candidates are required to answer multiple-choice questions, mainly from English language, basic math and general awareness. Written test is also a logistical challenge as the number of candidates appearing is too large and the fact that there is little time for preparation as the exact number of qualified candidates appearing in the written test is not known till the last day of PEMT. The TRP mandates that the written examination should also be above any suspicion of foul play. Therefore, the candidates are allowed to take the question paper with them along with a copy of the answers they have marked in the answer (OMR) sheet so that they can compare it with the correct answer key which is also put on the Delhi Police website preferably on the same day. The original answer sheet is read by the computer and there is no manual intervention in either evaluating the answers or tabulating the marks obtained by the candidates. This eliminates a lot of heart-burn on the part of the young candidates. After the written test result, the qualifying candidates are called for a medical examination by a doctor and are then issued an appointment letter asking them to join training.

The actual process of holding a written test for such a large volume of aspirants is a big drain on resources. Police officers are drawn from other units/districts to oversee and invigilate the examination. CCTVs and communication systems are installed to monitor the process. Adequate provisions are made for the convenience of the candidates and to ensure that the examination process is as smooth as possible.

Seeing the challenges of holding the written examination, there was a proposal to use technology by having online tests. After some deliberation and planning this has been implemented recently. This has enabled the written examination to precede the PEMT. Candidates for the post of Delhi police constables can take online tests at designated online test centres pan-India. However, the conduct of the physical test has remained the same albeit on a smaller scale as only those candidates are called for the PEMT who have qualified the online written test. Use of technology for recruitment seems the ideal way to put to rest the criticism of the earlier system.

BRAIN VERSUS BRAWN

It has been argued that police force needs constables who can think and act rather than those who are more physically fit. But, holding the PEMT to screen candidates appearing for the written test, eliminates the more cerebral aspirants in favour of the physically more accomplished ones. On the contrary, the system of online written test before the physical test leaves out physically more accomplished candidates in favour of the more intelligent ones who pass the written test. In my view, this 'brain versus brawn' argument is specious. We require both physically fit and mentally agile constabulary. It has been shown by various studies that physical fitness promotes mental faculties, rather than impeding them. Therefore, it all depends on what is more feasible and doable: PEMT before the written test or the other way around. Although these are early days to evaluate the new system, the use of online testing seems to be far more

SI Devi Prakash is an authority on recruitment process. He worked with his Inspector and ACP to adapt and implement the TRP in Delhi Police in 2010-12 period. Very knowledgeable about DP Recruitment Rules, he is called to assist in the recruitment process even after his retirement from service. He is a go-to man for any operational issue which might arise during the recruitment process or any legal issue thereafter.

convenient to administer provided proper infrastructure is available.

An alternate view: There is an alternate view that an all-India test be held for aspirants aiming to join the police or para-military force. The test, let us call it COPTEST, can be held by an accredited agency to assess the performance of each candidate and award scores which can remain valid for say 3 years or till the time one is within the prescribed age limit, whichever is less. During the validity period of the test score or the age limit, one can apply for a constable's job advertised by different police organizations in the country.

The states can have the physical endurance and measurement tests tailored to their own needs. The aspiring candidate with a valid COPTEST Score can apply individually and then take the PEMT conducted by those states. This would obviate the need for holding separate tests for each force and would be transparent and easy to administer. This would also delink the written from the PEMT, thus setting to rest the controversy whether physical or mental abilities should serve as the elimination parameter.

RECRUITMENT OF SUB-INSPECTORS

One of the most important ranks of the police hierarchy is the Sub-Inspector (SI). He or she has to be physically fit and intellectually accomplished to lead the lower rungs of the force, perform investigations and take quick decisions while handling crimes and mobs. The SI is the man at ground zero. It would not be an exaggeration to say that the fate and fortune of any police force depends on this rank. A wrong decision by the SI, whether during investigation of a case or while handling a law and order arrangement, can prove dearly for the organization as a whole. It is, therefore, in the interest of any police organization to invest heavily in the recruitment, training and up keep of this rank.

All organizations including police would like to take advantage of the knowledge and experience gained by the older generation of its employees. Their invaluable experience has to be combined with fresh ideas of the younger generation of employees joining the organization straight out of college. It is for this reason the composition of various ranks of officers reflects a mix of experience and fresh blood. For the post of SI, Delhi Police has a rule of 50-50. Half of the posts of SIs are filled up by promotion from the rank of ASI and the rest by direct recruitment.

In keeping with the job requirement of the SI, the recruitment process is more rigorous than that for the post of constable. Graduation is mandatory and the prescribed age-bracket of 20 to 25 years is also in line with the requirement of higher educational qualification. Delhi Police largely gets the recruitment of SIs conducted by the Staff Selection Commission (SSC), an agency of the Government of India which is entrusted with the recruitment of middle level non-gazetted staff, including SIs for the para-military forces. SSC conducts the written test first. Only those qualifying the test above a certain threshold are called for PEMT. Lately, however, a need has been felt to screen the applicants before the written test for which SSC conducts a preliminary test also. This has been necessitated by the fact that this is a combined examination for SIs of all Central Para-military Forces like CRPF, BSF and CISF as well as Delhi Police and CBI. For this reason, it attracts a large volume of applicants. The successful ones are allotted a service based on their merit and preference. The preliminary test, which is a computer-based examination, covers topics on Mental Reasoning, General Knowledge, Math and English. The final examination only has a paper in English. It goes without saying that Delhi Police, with the attraction of serving in the national capital, remains one of the favourite destinations for the aspirants of SI rank.

For the executive branch in Delhi Police, there are only three levels of direct entry—at the levels of lower subordinates—constables, upper subordinates (SI) and gazetted officers (ACPs and IPS officers). The other ranks are from promotion only. For instance, constables are promoted to the rank of Head Constables (HC), who in turn, are promoted to the next level of Assistant Sub-Inspector (ASI) and then to the rank of SI. As mentioned earlier, there is a 50% quota for promotion of ASIs to SIs; the remaining 50% is filled up by direct recruitment process enumerated above. The SIs in turn get promoted to the next rank of Inspector, which is the rank from which the post of Station House Officer (SHO) is filled.

INDIAN POLICE SERVICE

The IPS is an all-India service along with the Indian Administrative Service (IAS) and the Indian Forest Service (IFoS). The concept of an all-India service is that the members of these services are recruited by the Centre (Union Government in federal polity), but their services are placed under various State cadres, and they have the liability to serve both under the State, and under the Centre. Due to the federal polity of the country, this is considered one of the tools that make the Union Government stronger than State governments. Officers of these three services are governed by the All India Services Rules relating to pay, conduct, leave, various allowances, etc.

The Union Public Service Commission (UPSC) conducts the Civil Service Examination annually from which IPS officers as well as other all-India service officers and Central service officers are recruited. The IPS officers who get selected are allotted various State cadres. Earlier, IPS officers were allotted the Union Territory (UT) cadre which is now known as the AGMUT cadre after some UTs like Arunachal Pradesh Goa and Mizoram became full-fledged States and these got clubbed with the UT as a joint cadre. The AGMUT cadre IPS officers have to serve at any of these components, viz. Arunachal Pradesh, Goa, Mizoram and the seven UTs, viz. Delhi, Andaman and Nicobar Islands, Lakshadweep, Puducherry, Chandigarh, Daman & Diu, and Dadra and Nagar Haveli. Recently, the UTs of Jammu & Kashmir and Ladakh have been added to the AGMUT cadre.

There is another service, Delhi and Andaman & Nicobar Islands Police Service (DANIPS), which is also recruited from the same Civil Service Examination conducted by UPSC. However, this is not an all India service and is less preferred compared to the IPS. The officers of this cadre are also initially posted as an Assistant Commissioner of Police (ACP), same as the IPS officer, but being governed by the All India Service rules, the latter enjoys faster promotion. DANIPS is also a feeder service to the IPS, which means that these officers get inducted into the IPS at a subsequent date. The ACP is generally in-charge of a police subdivision which has the supervisory role over several police stations. The DANIPS officers can also be posted out to the UTs, not just Delhi and Andaman and Nicobar. In that sense, the name of the service is a misnomer, and a better name would be Union Territory Police Service (UTPS)

The **Civil Services Examination** (CSE) is a nationwide examination in India conducted by the Union Public Service Commission for recruitment to various Civil Services of the

Government of India, including the Indian Administrative Service (IAS), Indian Foreign Service (IFS), Indian Police Service (IPS), among others. It is conducted in three phases—a preliminary examination comprising two objective-type papers (general studies and aptitude test), a main examination comprising nine papers of conventional (essay) type, and a personality test (interview).The successful candidates are allotted service according to their rank and preference. Those who get the IPS are then allocated various State cadres, of which AGMUT is also one. Those who are interested in becoming a police officer under the Central Government join the DANIPS.

TRAINING

If the process of recruitment is like mining the ore, training is like smelting the ore to extract the metal. The ore itself is of no economic value but once the metal is extracted, it can be converted into very useful products. Needless to add, the process of smelting consists of physical and chemical actions before the metal is obtained. Similarly, police training involves both outdoor and indoor training, involving physical and academic process of imparting skills, knowledge and above all the attitude needed for a job as a law enforcement officer. Since the intake in the police department is at mainly three levels, namely Constables, SIs and GOs, the training requirements differ for each. But there are certain common ingredients, the foremost among which is physical training. A police officer at any level needs to be physically fit to face the rigours of long, arduous and risky work. Then there are some skills like weapon handling, field craft and tactics, communication, to mention just a few, which are essential for policemen and policewomen to discharge their duties with ease. They should have knowledge of laws—Penal Code, Evidence Act, Local and Special Laws. Then there are specialized areas like investigation techniques, forensics, IT and other important subjects like human rights, police management and so on, that are important ingredients of a police officer's tool-kit. The importance of training can be gauged from the fact that whenever there is a serious lapse on the part of police, media and society blame it on improper training. This is all the more reason that police training is given a very high priority in terms of resources and deployment of committed officers in training. It is pertinent that Police organizations including Delhi Police have a well-designed training strategy and the same is continuously upgraded to keep it up to date and relevant.

Police in India are commonly perceived to be unfair, corrupt, and inefficient. Research by J-PAL affiliates Abhijit Banerjee (MIT), Raghabendra Chattopadhyay (Indian Institute of Management), *Esther Duflo (MIT), and Daniel Keniston (Yale University) has shown that training in soft skills such as communication, stress management and leadership can facilitate community interaction and improve public perceptions of police performance. Following the evaluation, elements of training were scaled up across the police force in Rajasthan and incorporated into police training curriculum across India.*

*Accessed from https://*www.povertyactionlab.org

TRAINING OF CONSTABLES

Generally, for constable recruits there is more emphasis on physical training in keeping with the requirements of the job. The training period is less than a year, after which they are deployed in the field, initially in the armed battalions and later in police stations or other police units. Training of constables is rigorous in view of the fact that these are relatively young lot straight out of high school. As part of physical training they are made to do parade and other drills needed to build their physical fitness and stamina to enable them to perform the duties of a constable. They are also trained in unarmed combat and weapons. The recruits need to have sufficient grounding in the academic disciplines needed for discharging their duties in the police. Therefore, they are taught law subjects like Indian Penal Code (IPC), Criminal Procedure Code (Cr PC), Indian Evidence Act and some local and special laws. Among the local laws, Delhi Police Act 1978 from which Delhi Police draws its powers is an important area of study. They are also taught subjects like police sciences and police procedures and are even familiarized with computers and IT as these have become a mode of working in the police department.

The strictly regimented life in the recruit training school inculcates in the constables the virtues of leading a disciplined life and of obedience to seniors' orders. Most importantly, the recruits once out on the streets remain the most visible face of the police and are in constant contact with the community. When we talk of police-public relation, it is, generally, the constabulary we are dealing with. This makes it necessary that recruits are familiarized with behavioural aspects of police functioning. Consequently, they undergo intensive training on human rights, police-public relation, gender sensitivity and public interaction. They are also given grounding on body language and how to deal with public in general and weaker sections in particular. The recruits are subjected to a very strict regimen. Discipline is strictly enforced and any infraction attracts opprobrium. In case there is a serious misconduct or any action on his part which shows he is unsuitable for police service, the recruit can be terminated from service at the training school itself.

SUB-INSPECTOR'S TRAINING

If there is one rank which has many roles to play, it is the SI. He occupies the most important functional area of police hierarchy. He is the first, and the most important leader of the lower rungs—the constables and head constables who constitute the bulk of the police force. The SI is the kingpin of the preventive, investigative and regulatory aspects of law enforcement. The SI has immense powers in his arsenal including, the use of force, which can impact the citizens' fundamental rights. This rank is bestowed with powers of arrest, search and seizure, accepting bail, conducting inquests and summoning witnesses. In law and order *bandobast* his powers to regulate and control can be far reaching. This points out to the necessity of having very effective and comprehensive training curriculum for this rank.

In Delhi Police the SIs—both male and female—are trained at the department's own Police Training College where the probationer SIs spend one year. After successfully completing this part he spends a year in the Districts for field training. During the latter phase he gets an opportunity to apply his training school learnings in practice under the close supervision of SHOs at police stations and other senior officers of the district. His professional training emphasizes not only the theoretical aspects of law and procedures but of the practical aspects of police functioning like scientific aids in investigation, intelligence gathering, forensic science and important skills of detection and investigation. He is also trained in crowd management, traffic management and VIP security duties. The behavioural aspect of training for SIs is vast and includes training in human rights and in personal skills like patience, tact and problem-solving attitude. The SI is also taught counseling and negotiation skills, attributes he has to use extensively in his investigative and law enforcement functions. At the PTC he is exposed to various agencies like prosecution, courts, forensic labs, fire service, hospitals and mortuary with whom he or she has to deal regularly in the capacity of an IO.

Like in any other police rank, the requirements of discipline during the training stage are quite exacting. In case of any serious lapse like willful disobedience, gross misconduct, act of moral turpitude or any reason for which he is found unsuitable for police service, he can face disciplinary action or can even be terminated from service during training itself.

TRAINING OF INDIAN POLICE SERVICE OFFICERS

The Indian Police Service officers that have been selected through the All-India Civil Services Examination are trained at the SVP National Police Academy (SVPNPA), Hyderabad. Unlike the subordinate ranks such as constables, sub-inspectors and inspectors whose recruitment and training are the prerogative of the states and is done by respective state Director Generals of Police, the IPS is controlled by the Home Ministry of the Government of India. An officer of this service can only be appointed or removed by an order of the President of India.

The primary purpose of the training of IPS officers is to prepare leaders for the Indian police and to equip them to face law enforcement challenges of contemporary India. The National Police Academy organizes basic induction training of the IPS Probationers. The basic training aims to ensure that the Probationers acquire necessary knowledge, skills, attitudes, understanding and behaviour required for effectively discharging supervisory assignments in the successively senior ranks of police department. The 'Integrated Training' format being used at the Academy to impart training, focuses on fusion of three dimensions: Sensitization (personal and social), Orientation (ethical and legal) and Competency (domain and inter-segmental). The Academy further aims at nurturing human values in all its areas of activity to prepare Probationers not only to be good police professionals but also effective leaders.

The objective of basic course training is:

- Capacity building through the matrix of sensitization, orientation and competency.
- Imparting professional knowledge and understanding.
- Development of professional, behavioral and community skills.
- Nurturing human values, right attitudes and appropriate behavior in professional and personal life and inculcating sensitivity.
- Development of overall personality (character, habits, self-discipline, soft skills, norms, values, etiquette, etc.
- Transforming the Probationers into leaders of police stations and police districts.

The course curriculum of an IPS Probationer's training is very comprehensive and covers several contemporary topics. It is an intensive programme covering law subjects like IPC, CrPC, Evidence Act, Special Acts, and domain specific topics including Crime Prevention & Criminology, Investigation, Forensic Medicine and Forensic Science, Maintenance of Public Peace & Order and Internal Security. In keeping with the requirements of a modern police force there are courses on human rights and ethics and of Information and Communication Technology

(ICT). The fact that an IPS officer is a leader of the force, there are courses on leadership and police management. The Probationers are also exposed to academic inputs on evolution of the police force in India and contemporary global issues on law enforcement. The IPS induction training has several outdoor subjects including physical fitness, drills including sword drills, field craft, tactics and map reading. They also undergo programmes on equestrian, yoga and swimming. There is intensive training on essential skills like first aid and life-saving. The idea of the training is to turn them into well rounded individuals who can go on to make a competent officer and a good leader of the Indian police. The IPS officers undergo what is known as a sandwich course. After the first phase of nearly 10 months, they go to the cadres or States allotted to them. In the case of Delhi, the IPS officers allotted to the AGMUT cadre come to Delhi for 7 months in which they undergo training at the Police Training College in Delhi after which they undergo practical training in the districts. This period is mainly for familiarizing them with local conditions including local laws and contextual issues. They are also acquainted with the peculiarities of local police organization and local conditions. After this, for the second phase, the IPS Pro-bationers go back to National Police Academy, Hyderabad where they get an opportunity to reconcile the difference of theory imbibed in the first phase and share their experience gathered in the field during their stay in the cadre. After the second phase of training, the IPS officers go for a 1-week foreign attachment before returning to their respective states to join as Assistant Superintendents or Assistant Commissioners of Police.

One ceremony which is very sacred for all police forces is the Passing Out Parade (POP). When police officers, whatever their rank, complete their training an elaborate parade is held attended by the families of the graduating recruits as well as Senior Officers of Police Organizations. This is a very formal occasion and all uniformed personnel on their ceremonial uniforms including medals earned by them. The meritorious among the passing out batch are given awards. The passing out batch is also administered an oath of allegiance to the Constitution of India and to the police force by the head of the Training College or Academy.

Thus, we see that unlike other services, recruitment as well as training in the police organization is a process which is quite rigorous and designed to prepare the personnel for a challenging career ahead. They are also made aware of the fact that their actions would always remain under close scrutiny by various agencies and the community in general. Both the processes underline the importance of physical fitness and of professional competence required in their smooth job performance. Both recruitment and training require a perfect balance of outdoor and indoor processes. Any imbalance would lead to a deficit in physical or intellectual capabilities in the police force which affects delivery of service to the community. Being the capital of the country, Delhi cannot afford the luxury of a police force which is lacking in knowledge, skill or attitude of a good cop.

Chapter 4

One which Never Sleeps

The Police Station

A run-of-the-mill Bollywood movie invariably shows the police station (PS) as a place where all sinning takes place: rotund policemen accept bribes, arrogant criminals are let off after a VIP phone call, innocents tortured, and women raped. This negative portrayal has become so ingrained that ordinary people are afraid to even think of going to such a place and consider themselves lucky if they never get an opportunity to do so. To try and change this perception among people who have never set foot in a PS is a great challenge for even the best of marketing professionals.

But while most people shudder, there are many others belonging to the underprivileged sections of society and struggling against endemic scarcity in their day to day life that go to a police station often. Police is their only hope for interceding in disputes which invariably break out over basic necessities of life like clean drinking water, sanitation and jobs. In that sense, police is a comrade in arms in many of their struggles and police station is the place where they seek closure for many of their woes.

Contrary to its image, a police station is an institution which is open round the clock, and stands with the people in good times and bad, never tiring, never sleeping and never shutting its door. It is a place where systems and processes are working incessantly despite criticisms, censures, paucities, pulls and pressures. Let us take a look inside one to see for ourselves.

If you dispel your doubts and enter the PS, you will be met first by the Duty Officer (DO). He is like the front office manager you meet in a hotel lobby. He is the first point of contact for any visitor. He is a receptionist, records all happenings in the PS and keeps the Station House Officer (SHO) informed about the goings-on in the PS. He also receives complaints, attends to telephone calls, dispatches important messages to seniors, details personnel for various duties and, the most important of all, he records the First Information Report (FIR). Even supervisory officers visiting the PS show utmost regard for the DO, aware that this over-worked officer goes about his work silently and diligently, conscious of his onerous responsibilities and the consequences of any lapse. For example, if a person comes rushing to the PS in the night alleging a threat to his life, the DO has to respond with timely and effective action. If he fails to do so and the person is actually harmed, then the DO is held personally responsible for this lapse. This would also bring disrepute to the entire police force. It is not that people visit the PS only with a complaint about a crime. They do so for other sundry tasks, like passport verification, verification of their domestic help or tenants, or to obtain a police clearance certificate necessary to get a job, to mention just a few.

The various sub-parts within a PS and their work can best be understood if we take a live example. Suppose you visit a PS with a complaint about theft of a brief case from your parked car. You will first go to the Duty Officer who will listen to your verbal complaint and take down the description of the briefcase and the details of the incident. He would immediately initiate preliminary action like broadcasting the description of your briefcase over the police wireless system, thus alerting all checkpoints in Delhi about the theft. If any article of that description is intercepted by any checkpoint, it would be relayed back to the PS. Meanwhile, the DO assigns the case to an officer who is on stand-by for attending to an emergency. The Emergency Officer, as he is called, initiates the enquiry by first visiting the scene of crime. Before setting out for the crime scene he makes an entry about the gist of the complaint in the *Roznamcha* or the Station Diary. Once he reaches the spot, he verifies the incident, gathers some initial clues and makes a site map. He then records the statement of the complainant and sends it to the PS for registration of the FIR. Meanwhile, he continues with the investigation at the spot, examining the car for any clues like fingerprints. He also asks around for eyewitnesses of the crime.

Back at the PS, on receipt of the written complaint from the spot, the DO again gets into the act. He gets the First Information Report (FIR) registered citing the appropriate sections of law. This is done first by entering the gist of the complaint in the station diary. Thereafter, the complaint, as received from the officer on the spot, is reproduced verbatim in the FIR register. The FIR register is a permanent register of the PS and is never destroyed. The FIR number, an important reference point, starts and ends in a calendar year. For example, the cases of the year 2020 would be numbered 1/2020, 2/2020 and soon till the last case registered in that year. After the case is registered, a copy is given to the complainant and copies sent to some designated functionaries including the local magistrate's court.

Meanwhile, the Investigation Officer continues with the investigation at the spot and elsewhere wherever the lead takes him to. He records each step of investigation in the Case Diary. He prepares the site map, notes the details of property stolen, the circumstances of the incident, examines witnesses and suspects, picks up forensic clues, sends the same for opinion of experts, arrests the accused, seizes stolen property and takes any other step depending on the peculiarities of the case. Finally, as enumerated in earlier chapters, when the investigation is complete, he prepares the Charge-sheet and sends it to the court for trial.

Nathu Singh Yadav recently retired as an ASI. He was rendered medically unfit for active duty by an accident. The department allowed him to work as a Record Moharrir in a PS near his residence. A long stint in the record room made him a 'walking encyclopaedia.' With his vast knowledge of criminals He became an important member of every investigation team. 'The setting up of the manual system of record keeping was an act of genius and very difficult to replace even in this compute rage,' he says.

All the mandatory writing work associated with the investigation, from entry in the Daily Diary, to registration of FIR, writing of Case diaries to filing the Final report including the Charge-sheet is now an end to end computerized process. This has been made possible after the launch of CCTNS which stands for, Crime and Criminal Tracking Networks and System. In this, the entire crime and criminal records of all the police stations in the country would be entered in a giant database which would replace the hitherto manual system of recording and maintaining criminal records by each PS individually. Once it *goes live* for India as a whole, the system would replace the manual process of information storage, retrieval and sharing. This will be a revolutionary step for crime investigation in the country as any investigating officer throughout the country can access crime and criminal database. This is important as criminals move from place to place, in order to conceal their identity. This would become increasingly difficult for them now.

Record room: As soon as the case is registered, the PS Record room gets activated. In Delhi, the record is maintained according to Punjab Police Rule (PPR), which details the intricacies of criminal record-keeping. Even today the basic principles of criminal record keeping are followed in the police station record rooms. There are, in all, 25 PPR registers and several other registers which are maintained in the record room. In the pre-CCTNS days, the FIR written manually was christened Register no. 1 signifying the pre-eminence of the FIR and the fact that criminal record-keeping begins with registration of the case. The crime-scene or the place where the crime was committed is entered into the Beat-Book, which would show the beat within the PS jurisdiction. The compilation of such data over a period of time provides a marker to vulnerable areas of the PS for particular types of crime. This shows a direction of preventive action like beat patrolling, deployment of resources and intelligence collection. Case registration also necessitates an entry in a register titled 'Cases traced to the village', which means entering the name of the arrested person in the beat where he is residing. But as in the past and more so now, he may be a resident of another PS within the state or even outside the state. For such accused persons, there is a need to get the antecedents from the PS of which he is a resident. To get this done an Information Sheet is issued by the local PS in favour of the resident PS. The resident

PS is supposed to check the antecedents and criminal record from their own 'Cases traced to the village' register and send the other involvements of the accused to the PS of origin, which in turn updates its own record against the name of its criminal. The mechanism is quite robust on paper. However, being a manual system based on conventional mail delivery system it is plagued with obvious weaknesses. Apart from this, there is a problem of tracing the accused person's actual village and whether his family still lives there. This is because of the fact that there is a large migrant population that has no permanent home. Therefore, in a majority of cases the person does not get identified and it returns to the originating PS as 'untraced' or in old Urdu vernacular as '*adam tasdeeq*'.

The CCTNS system is expected to take care of this important issue. The database can be searched to find out about any criminal antecedents and present address of a suspect. On top of this, if the Aadhar number of a person, which is a unique identity number, is used for this purpose then it would make a serious dent on the tendency of criminals to hide their identity. The police will be able to find out the real criminal character of the accused who has committed a crime in the area. Society at large would also benefit as they would be sure of the person they are dealing with as employees, employers or in any business transaction. However, the access to Aadhar identification has not been given to law enforcement agencies (LEAs) so far.

After conclusion of an investigation the case is put in the court for trial. The Record *moharrir* keeps a tab on the progress of the case till the pronouncement of the final judgement. If the criminal is convicted by the court, this fact is entered in the Conviction register. Whatever the final verdict, the resident PS is also kept in the loop by sending the information sheet. It keeps updating the record of its residents committing crime outside its jurisdiction on the basis of information sheets received.

The trial process may not be as smooth as it may seem. The accused, if arrested, can be released on bail by the police or the courts and this fact is also entered in the bail register. This also has the name of the person who has stood surety for the accused so that he can be hauled up if the accused or undertrial, as he now is, absconds or jumps bail. If he actually does so, he is declared a Proclaimed Offender (PO) by the court. This fact is entered in a Proclaimed Offenders' register. Without confusing the reader any further about the intricacies of criminal record-keeping, I will just mention the most important of all the registers. This is the Register No. 10 which has a list of the Bad Characters (BC) of the area, meaning thereby, the criminals who commit a particular type of crime repeatedly. This register gives the colloquial name 'dus numbari' to a 'hardened' criminal. For each of these bad characters a History Sheet is maintained, detailing their movements in the PS area or even outside and all their criminal involvements. However, for opening a person's History Sheet, there are inbuilt procedural safeguards like seeking the approval of the DCP. This is because it entails surveillance of his activities which impinges on his Right to Privacy.

Malkhana: Coming back to the case example, if the police is able to recover your briefcase, you will have a view of the working of the *Malkhana*. The recovered briefcase is a case property and the *Malkhana* is a store-house of all such properties. You will be informed immediately by the IO and asked to come to the PS to identify your briefcase and its contents. In the *Malkhana* you will find your briefcase neatly arranged among other such case properties duly labelled with the FIR number. The *Malkhana Moharrir* is the main custodian, and he maintains a record of all such case properties. They also ensure that the case properties are remanded back to the owners so as to ensure that there is ample space in the *Malkhana* for newer properties. The properties which are taken by the owners have to be produced in the court as and when these are summoned. There are many case properties which are no longer in serviceable condition and remain unclaimed. In such cases the *Malkhana Moharrir* has to ensure that at the time of trial the properties are produced in the court. To do so in the condition in which it was seized remains a big challenge for the *Malkhana Moharrir.* Subsequently, it is also his responsibility to dispose of those properties that are no longer required by any legal authority. This is done according to a set procedure so as to make sure that those properties which are still required for the due process of law are not destroyed or disposed of by mistake. Apart from case properties, the *Malkhana* is a storehouse of government properties like arms and ammunitions, cash and other valuables. The *Moharrir* is also responsible for issuing to the PS staff, equipments as basic as ropes, ladders and torches as well as sophisticated items like metal detectors, explosive detectors, arms and ammunitions. In a PS, this may happen several times a day and therefore the place is a very busy one.

Lock-up and sentry: The lock-up is an essential part of the police station and perhaps the most feared. On any normal day, the police station arrests one or more persons who are kept in the lock-up. A person can be put behind bars only with a reason which has to be recorded in the Roznamcha or the Station Diary. Arrests can be made in the course of a criminal investigation or in several other matters like an absconder from an earlier case or someone breaking the peace. Within 24 hours he has to be produced before a magistrate who may release him on bail or order his further detention which can either be a police remand or a judicial remand. When the arrested person is on police remand, he is kept in the PS lock-up unless he is taken out for the purpose of investigation, like for example, identification of a scene of crime, recovery of a case property or arrest of an accomplice. An armed sentry is posted outside the lock-up for security and safe custody of the inmate. There are separate lock-ups for female inmates and a lady officer should be in her presence for the entire duration of her stay in the PS.

There are other safeguards also in the statutes as well as various court rulings which list out the mandatory steps taken before, and after, the arrest of a person. All these are meant to ensure that the basic human rights are not trampled by the police at any stage. This is also one of the main reasons why Evidence Act does not allow the police to extract confession from the accused since it is not of any evidentiary value in the ensuing court trial. The safeguards for calling a female to the station, leave alone arresting her is too strict and the consequences of violation too severe. A professional police officer makes sure that all the mandatory conditions for handling a suspect or an accused are adhered to in letter and spirit.

Beat policemen: The description so far seems to suggest that the PS is an officer-oriented place with investigation being the most important function of the police. This is not so, and the personnel of the station predominantly consists of the lower subordinates (HCs and Constables). Investigation of crime is an activity which takes place after the occurrence. More important is the prevention of crime. This is done in Delhi, primarily but not solely, through beat policing. As stated in an earlier chapter, the PS area is divided into beats, each of which may have more than one beat constable headed by an

HC. Their duty is to patrol the beats on foot. In earlier times beats consisted of a group of villages. Each village used to have a chowkidar or local watchman. With urbanization and increase in population the beats have shrunk in physical size but increased in population density as well as complexity. The purpose of beat policing is two-fold, first, to remain visible in the area which is a serious deterrent to crime. Secondly, the beat officers have to collect local intelligence. For this he needs a lot of ingenuity. He has to mingle with the residents, shopkeepers, hawkers and other persons in his beat. His capability depends on whether he is able to gain confidence of the people and whether he is able to develop a relationship of mutual trust with them. But most importantly, he uses his common sense. The beat policing system is a very effective mechanism for crime prevention as local intelligence is helpful in monitoring movements of suspicious people in the beat and apprehending the offenders even before he is able to commit the crime. In the crime prevention role, a beat officer is supposed to keep a tab on the bad characters and listed ruffians of the area to ensure they do not indulge in law breaking. He also develops sources for collecting local intelligence. In the present times the beat officers have also been assigned several specific functions like checking of banks, schools and visiting

ASI Hansraj, now in the PCR, was a very accomplished beat officer in the old Delhi area in the late nineties. Recalling his days as a beat constable he says people would consider him a family member and was often called to mediate in husband-wife feuds also. 'It was one of the best times of my career as a cop. I realised how much a beat officer can do in increasing the happiness of ordinary people.' He was so popular in the beat that on his routine transfer to another PS, people came as a delegation to request for his retention in the area. As a special case the demand was accepted.

senior citizens daily. They are also held responsible for occurrence of any preventable crime in their beats.

Every morning the SHO holds a briefing of beat officers in the PS before they are sent out to their beats. They are also given specific duties everyday depending on the need which keeps changing from time to time. For example, during festivals and national holidays like Republic Day and Independence Day, they have to keep an eye on terrorist activities and for this, they have to perform mandatory checks in the area, like markets, guest-houses and hotels. The SHO also holds a de-briefing session every afternoon to take note of any situation which needs his intervention or requires further action on his part. The beat officers go to their beats in the evening also when there is heavy rush in the area. They have to keep a record of their daily activities in their 'beat-book' which also lists all important duty points, names of active criminals, BCs and local contacts. (Recently, an electronic version called the eBeat-Book has been launched with the express purpose of doing away with manual process of entry and retrieval of beat-level data). Beat policing is not just a day-time phenomenon. One beat constable is on night-shift patrolling his beat, albeit, supported by additional night duty staff from the PS.

On the midnight of July 2, 1995, Delhi police constable Abdul Nazir Kunju on night patrol saw smoke emanating from the open-air Bagiya Restaurant. He got suspicious and scaled the hotel's boundary wall to enter the premises. 'Something big' was burning in a tandoor (a clay oven) in the restaurant.

That 'something big' turned out to be the body of Naina Sahni (29), who was allegedly killed by her husband Sushil Sharma, a prominent Delhi politician.

The presence of mind shown by the beat policeman helped solve the infamous Tandoor Murder case.

But beat policing is not the only crime prevention measure in the tool-kit of the police. There are also other measures like mobile patrolling, physical checking at check points, surveillance over potential criminals, monitoring the activities of active and past criminals, rounding up of ruffians, preventive arrests and evidence-based area patrolling, to mention just a few. The launch pad of all such activities is the PS and the superintendence and direction of the SHO and other senior supervisory formations are crucial in this. Any lack of strategic focus in this starts showing in an uptick in crime. Also, number of complaints and PCR calls by the public increase.

Officers of the PS: Station House Officer (SHO) is the leader of the PS and it is up to him to decide how he deploys his manpower and other resources to meet the law enforcement objectives. He is assisted by two other Inspectors, one for investigation and the other for anti-terrorist operations. But in the present scenario such neat compartmentalization of responsibilities is not possible and they are also used for other jobs as and when required. For beat policing also the SHO is assisted by several SIs or ASIs who are designated Division officers. Each division within the PS area is a collection of few beats. The division officer is the leader of his division and supervises the functioning of the beat officers under him. Any complaint or matter received at the PS pertaining to a division is marked to the concerned officer who may take the help of the beat staff for dealing with the matter. If there is any serious crime, especially a property crime, it is assigned to the division officer who takes up investigation and mobilizes local intelligence and other inputs to try and solve the case.

Law and order: Apart from routine work of prevention and investigation of crime, a PS has to deal with law and order duties. These are basically police arrangements or *'bandobast'* dealing with a congregation or assembly which may be lawful or unlawful, peaceful or violent. The reason for the gathering is important, which may be foreseen or unforeseen. For example, the congregation can be a cricket match, fair, religious or cultural event, or a protest movement, dharna or agitation. But for all these events the PS has to make proper police arrangements so that there is no breakdown of law and order in the area. PS is the lead agency for arrangements and depending on the size and sensitivity other specialized agencies like Traffic police, Special Branch and VIP Security are pressed into service. In such events the SHO has to mobilize all his resources so that the events are conducted peacefully and smoothly. In unforeseen events like a major crime or a snap demonstration by a group or even a terrorist attack, the capabilities of the Police Station as well as the leadership qualities of the SHO are tested. Such events also impart a lot of organizational learning in crowd-management, tact and patience which Delhi Police has accumulated in plenty over the years. Generally, good police officers especially the SHOs have a contingency plan ready for their respective areas. These are not one-size-fits-all plans but are formulated keeping in mind

The ACP was taking a random feedback from the names entered in the Women's Help-desk Register which he was reviewing. He spoke telephonically to Mrs. Aparna Kapoor. She had visited the Hauz Khas Police station the previous week for lodging a police report on her lost passport which was needed to get a duplicate issued from the Passport office. Never having entered a PS before she was full of apprehension on what she would face there, the stereo-type of the police playing in her mind. 'But I was pleasantly surprised. A young lady officer came to me as soon as I had entered. She asked me the purpose for visiting the station and with a smile she got the work done without any fuss. I was out of the place in no time with a police report in my hand. 'One visit and she was forced to change her impression of the police and the police station.

the specific context of the PS. The odds against a mishandled law and order situation are very high. Many heads have rolled in the past for not handling the situation effectively.

Inspection of PS: From earlier times and to this day, there is a six-monthly inspection of every PS in Delhi by one Gazetted officer. In such inspections the entire functioning of the PS is reviewed in depth including cases registered, quality of records and registers maintained, the upkeep of case properties, quality of investigation undertaken and preventive efforts of the PS. The inspection reports are taken very seriously, and any shortcomings pointed out are acted upon and corrective action taken.

Smart Police Station: In the age of smart phones, smart cards and smart everything it is natural that the police station also turns smart. The smartness of a police unit is not just in terms of outward appearance but in their attitude and functioning. In Delhi, the PSs have got a new look in terms of infrastructure, facilities and vehicles. They have also been mandated to be more citizen-friendly in their working. For example, these days when you enter a Police Station in Delhi there is a Public Facilitation officer who is there to help you in getting your work done expeditiously and without hassle. Similarly, there is a Women's Help-desk where a lady officer assists any lady visiting PS. She also records this in a register which is routinely checked by the SHO and other supervisory officers to ensure that all female visitors are attended to properly and in a sensitive manner.

In the late1980s, Delhi Police underwent some sort of a renaissance when they realized the importance of brand-image and the dividends of having a better public perception. Earning the trust of the citizens would be a win-win situation for both. People would feel more relaxed in approaching the police and the police would get the much-needed cooperation in its preventive and investigative work. Ever since then, they have endeavoured to improve this image through better police-public relations. Lately, they have started using technology in a big way so that more people-friendly services can be provided. For instance, one can register an eFIR for a cyber offence or a vehicle theft or an online report for a missing documents, without physically going to the PS. They can make a complaint against any person or police personnel through an online portal Integrated Complaint Management System (ICMS). The citizen-centric approach of Delhi police allows them to analyze the pain-points of the people in an effort to minimize them by reforming their attitude and processes.

Not only technology but there is a serious outreach programme unfolding these days. Police stations have *open days* when they invite school children, show them around, give them gifts and organize painting and quiz competitions. This is meant to create a positive impact in young minds and to enhance the image of Police. On Saturdays, an Alternative Dispute Redressal camp is held in every PS to settle minor disputes by calling and mediating between the rival parties. Police stations have started various other outreach programmes like self-defence training for girls, medical camps, career counseling, skill development and the like. Lately, Delhi Police has tied up with the Government of India to initiate the Yuva programme for skilling unemployed youths of the area. In the long run, such programmes would not only enhance its image but would also prevent young adults to enter a world of crime. If Delhi Police consistently works in this direction, then a time would come when even a school child who has lost his book would first take his complaint to the Police Station rather than to his mother.

CHAPTER 5

Keep the Wheels Running

The Traffic Police

If there is one organ of Delhi Police that touches the life of nearly every citizen of the city, it is the Traffic Police. Other units of the police either do not come in contact with the public or do so only when a crime is committed. On the other hand, any citizen who leaves his home in the morning for work or recreation is affected by traffic on the roads and, therefore, by implication, with the performance of traffic police. The latter has to ensure safe and smooth flow of men and materials in the city, all day and night. In that sense it keeps the wheels of the city moving; and that too in a proactive rather than a reactive manner.

But are the traffic police really needed? What if they are pulled out of the system? Will the city grind to a halt? Well, there is a view that if people come out of their homes, they will necessarily go back regardless of traffic police. However, imagine reaching an intersection and finding the traffic lights not working. In the peak hours of the day, you will encounter a massive traffic jam. What if you face the same situation at the next, and the traffic signal after that as well? One can imagine the plight of the people. They would, of course, reach home ultimately, but after a very frustrating day where they may miss their flights, their classes and their appointments. Therefore, it is hard to imagine a city like Delhi without the assuring presence of the Traffic Police.

At a time when India is trying to get into the globalization mode, there is a view that India has the potential to be among the leading nations of the world. On the other hand, there is also a view that certain critical bottlenecks are an impediment to our progress. Infrastructure is one such constraint. Such factors not only restrict the various forces of change but also give the impression that we are unable to take remedial measures for such a basic problem. This feeling is exacerbated by the fact that even the capital city of India, where the strategy of development is being formulated, is in the stranglehold of such a compelling constraint. The first impression that a person visiting Delhi gets is one of utter chaos, with haphazard traffic movements, congestion and filthy grey smog enveloping the city. The average citizen increasingly feels that the city has crossed the threshold of livability.

Unprecedented population pressure has led to the acute overburdening of civic and physical infrastructure. According to the 1991 census, Delhi's total population was 94.20 lakhs. Today, it has crossed a hundred million, having registered a growth rate of over 300% since 1951. Along with the population explosion, there has been a tremendous increase in the number of registered motor vehicles in the city. With increase in economic activity and availability of several modes of travel, mobility in Delhi has increased. The city's metro system is already handling the enormous demand for public transport. Despite that, the number of personalized modes of transport has increased tremendously. Road capacity, obviously, has failed to keep pace with the increase in road traffic.

This development has led to the overburdening of the road network and its associated problems. There has been a growing incidence of traffic congestion on the major arterial roads. The travel speed of traffic has reduced significantly leading to delays and wastage. There has been a rapid increase in the number of accidents—both non-fatal and fatal. Delhi, according to some studies, has become a very unsafe place to live.

TRAFFIC SCENARIO IN DELHI

Every day approximately 2000–2100 new vehicles are registered in Delhi. At last count, there were approximately 1.15 crore vehicles in the city of which approximately 32 lakhs are four wheelers and 76 lakh two wheelers. The total vehicle population in Delhi is more than the combined total of the three metros: Mumbai, Chennai and Kolkata. It is true that all these vehicles are not on the roads at the same time, but it gives a fair indication of the congestion on the roads, keeping in mind the fact that vehicles from the neighbouring satellite towns in the NCR also enter the city, carrying the large floating population daily. Several studies conducted to assess the extent of congestion have painted a very grim picture of precious time wasted on the roads on account of traffic delays and low average speeds in the city. This is also contributing in no small measure to the problems of air and sound pollution. The city also has a very high traffic accident figure. In the year 2019, there were a total of 5,610 traffic accidents in the city, one-fourth of which were fatal in which 1,463 people lost their lives. Even though the statistics of fatal accidents are falling every year, the number is still very high for any civilized society.

Apart from accidents, another factor that makes Delhi very unsafe is pollution. It has earned the dubious distinction of being the third most polluted city in the world. The level of **Suspended Particulate Matter** (SPM) has been measured at 460 mg/cubic meter, which is much higher than the safe level of 200 fixed by WHO. Also, the noise levels in many parts of the city has crossed 82 decibels, which is a cause for concern

Besides this, parking in Delhi is a big problem, magnified by a lack of policy in this regard. Kerb-side parking takes up valuable road-space. The problem is compounded by the erratic behaviour of road-users. Traffic rules and safety norms are flouted with impunity, leading to a chaotic scene on the roads. Moreover, there is an enormous presence of pedestrians who form a major chunk of road-users in Delhi. There is rampant encroachment on the roads by hawkers, shopkeepers and squatters that hinder the free flow of traffic.

The citizens of Delhi are aware of the above-mentioned problems plaguing the city. But they wonder if anything can be done to improve the situation. Therefore, the immediate task for Traffic Police is to make Delhi a safe and healthy place to stay. This would also convey the message that we are serious about tackling this serious problem, which in turn would give a big boost to our efforts to modernize and globalize India. Therefore, it is imperative that a semblance of order is brought on Delhi's roads by disciplining the road-users and making them aware of the traffic rules and safety norms.

The main objective of traffic management is to ensure a safe and smooth flow of traffic on the road network. This basically means dealing with three major problems, viz. congestion, accidents and pollution. Till the mid 1980s, the traffic management machinery had not been under so much pressure to perform. Problems were neither large in dimension nor complicated in nature. Traffic managers relied more on practical rules of thumb. Their decisions were reactive in nature. But, with the new challenge that modern traffic-transportation scenario has thrown up, the old paradigms have become outdated, and the earlier techniques of traffic management do not seem to be effective any longer. Consequently, a fresh proactive approach to traffic management has been adopted in which technology plays a very important part.

In Delhi, accidents are a major area of concern. In fact, the city has begun to be rated as one of the most unsafe places in the world. This makes it imperative for the entire traffic management set-up to take a fresh look at the problem and take remedial measures fast. Otherwise, an unimaginable loss of society's precious resources would occur which can never be recovered. An accident reduction strategy is an important part of Delhi Traffic Police's charter of responsibilities.

It would, however, be unfair to judge the performance of the unit only on the accident rate or other traffic problems like traffic congestion or pollution. There are numerous factors causing accidents, for example, improper road engineering, poor lighting, easy availability of driving licenses, ignorance of rules, unsafe driving, to name just a few. Similarly, traffic congestion is caused by an overburdened public transport system, pre-dominance of personal vehicles, unplanned urbanization and multiplicity of modes of transport, including slow-moving vehicles. The readers can see that Traffic Police have no control over most of these factors. With limited resources they cannot educate and re-educate the vast number of drivers who own driving license but have had no formal education let alone traffic training. During issuing of license, the process of testing of driving skills is not rigorous. There is no tradition of proper driving on the roads where knowledgeable drivers are far outnumbered by illiterate ones. The traffic policemen are themselves outnumbered by the number of vehicles on the roads which is increasing at a galloping pace with rise in people's income and easy availability of car loans.

DELHI TRAFFIC MANAGEMENT SYSTEM

Traffic management involves a systematic regulation of the pattern of traffic flow so that the most optimal use is made of the road system, besides reducing the conflict between vehicles and other road-users including pedestrians. Modern traffic management basically aims at eliminating delays, curbing pollution and reducing accidents.

Some of the traffic management techniques used in Delhi are as follows:

Enforcement: The enforcement of traffic rules and regulations is an important constituent of what is called the three E's of traffic management, viz. Enforcement, Engineering and Education. Enforcement can be divided into two functions: Regulation and Prosecution.

Traffic regulation is basically the control and regulation of traffic flow within the road network. Regulation is done in order to make it smooth and safe. In Delhi, traffic regulation is done both manually and non-manually. In manual regulation, the traffic police personnel, basically the lower subordinates (Head Constables and Constables) supported by the Delhi Home guard constables manually control the traffic at junctions. In non-manual regulation, traffic is regulated using traffic signals. Traffic signals and manual regulation are not mutually exclusive. In fact, the former is supplemented and supplanted by the latter from time to time.

Prosecution is basically the legal enforcement of traffic rules. Any road user who violates a traffic rule, under various provisions of law, is prosecuted for the offence. This instrument of traffic management has the force of law behind it. It is for this reason that traffic police has to interface with the judiciary. At the time of prosecution, the offender is given the option of either paying the fine on the spot if he admits his fault or challenge it in court. In the latter case his *challan*, as the traffic ticket is known in Delhi, is sent to the Court. The violator has to appear before the magistrate who decides whether to fine or let off. Prosecution of offences cannot be done by the lower subordinates (HCs and Constables). Traffic Inspectors (TIs) who head a traffic police circle and the SIs and ASIs, who are called Zonal Officers (ZOs) mainly perform prosecution duties.

Unless one is posted in a specialized unit of police like traffic, one is not aware of the talent that abounds there. Policemen specialize in very niche areas. Sub Inspector Radhey Shyam was an officer who had an innate talent for traffic education. He used to visit schools and colleges to mobilize students and educate them in traffic rules and safe driving behaviour. He had trained thousands of students for creating the Road Safety Patrol, which used to assist Delhi Traffic Police in traffic regulation. Very popular among students, the officer was very creative and an able organizer who held fabulous events and awareness programmes for promoting road safety.

Engineering: Traffic engineering is an important aspect of traffic management. It deals with the application of technology, and engineering tools and techniques for the improvement of traffic flow on road networks in order to facilitate safe and efficient movement of people and goods. Delhi Traffic Police has only a recommendatory role in traffic engineering. Various civic agencies like NDMC, MCD, PWD, CPWD, etc. carry out the work of traffic engineering, whether it is improvement of road geometrics, constructing additional roads or provision of facilities like speed-breakers, street lighting etc. But they often seek the suggestions of the traffic police.

Education: Traffic education and awareness of road users is an important but least recognized component of traffic management. In our country a vast population has not undergone any formal education and to expect them to understand traffic rules and regulations is unrealistic. Moreover, they obtain a driving license from the licensing authorities without undergoing a rigorous testing process. When these drivers with poor driving skills and knowledge, start driving, they find drivers with similar capabilities on the road. Therefore, the roads also do not give them a conducive learning environment. In such a situation, traffic education undertaken by schools and other agencies assumes a very important role. However, in Delhi, the Traffic Police have to carry out this onerous task. There is a separate the Road Safety Cell for traffic education which undertakes programmes to increase the awareness of target groups of road-users. Various methods are adopted like formal and informal instruction in schools and colleges, Traffic Training Parks, Exhibition Vans, Road Safety Patrols and the use of mass media for generating awareness of traffic rules and safety.

Special Measures: Various other measures are adopted by the Traffic Police to ensure safe and smooth traffic flow. Examples are introduction of traffic circulation schemes, like one-way streets, contra-flows, traffic-calming measures, etc.

Apart from the usual traffic management function, there are other important duties performed by the Delhi Traffic Police. These are VVIP duties, like routes and traffic arrangements during processions, rallies, festivals and other events. These duties and arrangements take up a considerable amount of time of the traffic personnel and though they cannot be considered normal traffic duties, these are nevertheless an essential part of the system.

Several factors interact to create the traffic eco-system. These are:

1. Road users like pedestrians, cyclists or those using either private or public transport.

2. Different types of public transport like bus, rail or metro.

3. Vehicles on roads, both passenger and goods.

4. The road environment: Physical aspects of road, lighting, etc. and the legal and regulatory framework.

'The Traffic SMS Alert service is yet another initiative by the Delhi traffic police in which the registered users will get alerts via SMS regarding traffic situation like congestion points, water-logging, rallies, processions, traffic restrictions, accidents, breakdown of vehicles, etc. 'The service was launched in association with the Ministry of Communication and Information Technology. This is not the first time the Delhi Police tried to connect with the masses through the use of technology. Back in 2010, they had launched their own Facebook and Twitter accounts to coincide with the Commonwealth Games. The service was very well received by the people of the city and many people were more than happy to give suggestions to the police through these two accounts.

Adapted from www.digit.in

For effective management, traffic managers have to consider all these influences. Delhi has a multiplicity of agencies each concerned with different aspects of the traffic system. It is for this reason that the Delhi Traffic Police has to coordinate with several agencies, as varied as Municipal authorities like NDMC, MCDs, departments like PWD, Telephones, DDA, State Transport Department and other transport providers like DTC, DMRC and Railways. In addition, Delhi Traffic Police has to deal with some other agencies including private ones, like the company entrusted with installation and maintenance of traffic signals. They also have to interface with the judiciary. Prosecution of traffic offenders, which is an important component of traffic management, is to be carried out strictly in accordance with law. Law gives an opportunity to the offender to be heard. At the time of prosecution, the offender is given the option to either admit his guilt and pay the penalty on the spot (called 'compounding' of offence) or contest the *challan* in a court of law. The basic laws for traffic in Delhi are the Motor Vehicles Act, the Central Motor Vehicles Rule and the Delhi Police Act with various Regulations. However, compounding is not allowed for all offences.

There is a misconception about prosecution of traffic offenders (called *challans*) which needs to be cleared. The Traffic Police do not have any quota for traffic *challans* which they have to achieve. They are not an agency for revenue collection and hence they do not have any revenue collection target to achieve unlike the Income Tax or GST department of the government. They also do not get any share of the revenue collected. It all goes to the government treasury. The budget of the Traffic Police does not depend on the quantum of their prosecution fines collected. Therefore, the sole legal need for *challaning* a traffic offender is to prosecute him or her for traffic violations and in the process, to try and correct their future road behaviour.

The magnitude of traffic problem is such that the traditional approach to traffic management is no longer effective. What is needed is a fresh approach which is more innovative and strategic. Seeing the recent developments in the field of Information and Communication Technology (ICT) as well as other areas of technology, there is enormous potential to revolutionize the way we look at things and the way we solve our problems. Any sustainable solution for traffic problems must be able to exploit the potentials of technology.

TECHNOLOGY

Among police forces in India, Delhi Police and especially its Traffic wing was one of the first to adopt technology. Apart from generic products like vehicles and communication, the system of traffic signals which replaced manual regulation of traffic at junctions can be considered as the earliest technological device to be used by police. Traffic flow pattern on any road, as anyone can experience, changes with the time of the day. The 'traffic controller' which controls the traffic flow at a traffic junction can be pre-programmed to change the cycle time based on the which arm of the junction has more traffic at a particular time of the day. This feature clears the traffic on each arm of the junction by giving it more 'green' time. These days there are very sophisticated Intelligent Traffic Systems (ITS) which capture real-time traffic data by sensors on the road that is processed by sophisticated computers telling the signals which arm should be green and for what duration. Apart from traffic signal controllers there are other technology-based devices used by the Delhi Traffic Police. For prosecution they also use Radar Guns which check the speed of vehicles and help prosecute the drivers that violate speed limits. Then there are automatic cameras installed at traffic junctions and other places which record over-speeding or red-light violations automatically. These also capture the images which help as evidence in prosecuting these vehicles. In addition, there are CCTV cameras installed at various roads which help in monitoring the traffic situation from remotely located control rooms. Some of these cameras also have the Automatic Number Plate Recognition (ANPR) systems which read the vehicle number plates, compare it with the database and help identify traffic violators as well as car borne criminals.

ORGANIZATIONAL SETUP

Even though Delhi Traffic Police performs a very specialized role, they remain an integral part of Delhi Police. The personnel are drawn from the parent unit and they go back to it after their tenure is complete. The same service rules with regard to promotion, reward and punishment, etc. apply to them. The Commissioner of Police is the overall head of Delhi Police and he is assisted by a Special Commissioner of Police for traffic matters who in turn are assisted by other senior formations. The jurisdiction of Delhi is divided into Traffic Circles which are grouped in Districts and several districts make up a Range, each headed by a Deputy Commissioner of Police. Presently, the traffic police is divided into 12 districts, each headed by an Assistant Commissioner of Police. Each district in turn is divided into four or five traffic circles, each headed by a Traffic Inspector (TI). In every Traffic Circle, there are 7-8 ZOs as well as lower subordinates (Head Constables and Constables). Delhi Home guards also provide constables for traffic duties. In the Traffic Police HQ there is a DCP assisted by several ACPs, each heading a separate unit like, ACP/Road Safety, ACP/Traffic Engineering and ACP/Public Relations and Grievances. There is a large secretarial staff organized into different branches like Accounts, Personnel, Administrative Branch, etc. connected with the Traffic HQ.

Day in and day out, Delhi Police and particularly its Traffic wing is under a close scrutiny by the media, judiciary, government agencies and the common citizens. Everyone has some suggestion for improving the traffic situation and it is proffered to the Traffic Police since it is the only visible and omnipresent agency for traffic management. But the fact remains that they have only two instruments at their disposal- traffic regulation and prosecution of traffic violators.

Regulation of traffic is constrained by the road space and prosecution by the number of officers that can prosecute. Despite its shortcomings, Delhi Traffic Police, as the only agency for traffic management in the city, is performing efficiently within the given resources. Its efforts have at least prevented a total break-down of the traffic-transportation system in the city. In fact, the manpower resources of Delhi Traffic Police are of a high quality and given a proper organizational and operational environment, the same manpower can deliver even more efficiently. In the end I would also like to mention that the recent talk of increasing the amount of traffic fines through an amendment in the traffic laws is long overdue and would definitely lead to an improvement in the behaviour of road users in Delhi also. However, the new fine structure would have to be properly dovetailed with a proper strategy of traffic enforcement by the Delhi Traffic Police.

Chapter 6

Sentinels of the City

Special Branch and Special Cell

A police organization mirrors the society it serves. With increasing complexity in the capital city, Delhi Police has, over time, become a complex organization. It has hived off several aspects of law enforcement from the police station and created new units and outfits for performing varied tasks. With a proliferation of all types of crime and criminals, collection of intelligence became too cumbersome and technical to be left to the Police Station. Added to it is the requirement of policing a democratic and politically conscious society where staging protests are ingrained in our collective psyche. Above all, terrorism and its changing nature throw up a completely new challenge to policing the capital of the country. Two units in Delhi Police that act as sentinels of the city while remaining in the background are the Special Branch and the Special Cell. The latter originated as a specialized wing of Special Branch but has now developed into a full-fledged unit. It would not be off the mark to say that intelligence collection is the mainstay of both these organizations.

Special Branch

Special Branch is primarily tasked with collection of all forms of intelligence used for the maintenance of law and order in the city. Law enforcement agencies cannot work in a vacuum. The main operational challenge for a police organization is to prioritize the deployment of its scare resources, especially manpower. It needs intelligence inputs for assessing the temporal and spatial requirements of law enforcement. A city like Delhi has several law and order challenges happening on a daily basis. There are various organized groups like industrial workers, students, traders, political and social organizations, and various NGOs. It is possible that they become restive and hold rallies, demonstrations, strike, sit-ins or other types of protest movements in any part of the city, pressing for their demands. It becomes incumbent upon the police to collect all possible intelligence about the event well in advance. For this, the Special Branch deploys its 'sources' or assets, so as to collect all available intelligence inputs, collate, classify and analyze them. The actionable inputs are then forwarded to all the law enforcement agencies on the ground. Apart from the concerned police stations, these include Police Control Room (PCR), Traffic Police, Security Unit and Railways & Metro, all of which need good and reliable intelligence inputs for managing a law and order issue.

A police station has to make arrangements for crowd control and maintenance of law and order. Traffic police have to pitch in with a traffic plan for smooth arrival and dispersal of the crowd such that there is minimum dislocation of the general traffic system and therefore of public inconvenience. PCR has to sensitize the Operation Room regarding any developing situation on the ground with law and order implications. They also deploy their PCR vans at strategic locations for visibility and quick response in any eventuality. Railways and the Metro Police have to monitor the additional Railways and the Metro Police have to monitor the additional flow of crowd for the demonstration or rally. The Security unit of the Delhi Police which provides security to a protected person (PP) is also involved in this exercise as very often such PPs attend and address these public gatherings and their personal security is to be ensured. The Special Branch also has to separately conduct an exercise to determine the threat perception for the PP and whether it would be safe to bring him or her to the place of function. It is incumbent upon the law enforcement outfits to study and analyze the intelligence inputs, adapt these in their domains and undertake proper planning and implementation of arrangements so as to handle the event without disruption of the law and order situation.

The intelligence collected has to be very elaborate. It should include the background of the organizations involved, the type of event, its size, composition and leadership. Description of the leadership should include their past reputation and all other relevant facts which may determine their probable action. Do they have a good control over their followers? Do they provoke the crowd to break the law and indulge in violence? Whether they follow non-violent methods of protest and heed the directions of the police or are they rabble rousers? Then, there should be accurate information about the crowd, their background and past behaviour. From where have they been drawn and how are they expected to behave as a crowd? From the law and order point of view, are there any trigger points which can provoke the crowd to break rules and go berserk? What is the extent to which they can go? How is the crowd mobilized? The issue for which the crowd is assembling is also important from law and order angle. For example, if it is an emotive issue, the crowd is expected to be very volatile and police should be on their toes to avoid any trigger points.

The above description of role of the Special Branch pertains to big rallies or demonstrations that have a larger dimension and potential for law and order breakdown in the city. But there are smaller events also arising out of routine issues which have ramifications for day-to-day law enforcement. For example, a local issue like electric load shedding in a locality in the peak of summer leading to a ransacking of the electricity supply office can be relevant for the Branch. The demolition of unauthorized structures from a public land, the removal of hawkers from pavements or even an incident like a murder or traffic accident can have potential law and order ramifications. Special Branch has to remain abreast of all such issues and keep analyzing them from a law and order perspective. This makes its work that much more painstaking and needing meticulous real-time intelligence gathering on the ground.

The following facts would give an idea of the workload of Special Branch. In the year 2019, there were as many as 6,929 events which included 768 demonstrations, 1,272 dharnas, 404 processions, 1,044 meetings, 386 strikes, 927 rallies/marches, and 2,128 miscellaneous matters such as union elections, press conferences, protests and general body meetings in the city.

Accessed from Delhi Police Annual Report 2019

Special Branch also comes into action during seemingly innocuous events which have no perceptible relationship with the law and order landscape. For example, the Branch recently had to keep a close vigil over the implementation of the covid pandemic protocols like wearing of mask, social distancing etc. by various field units of Delhi police. Also in the aftermath of demonetization when huge queues collected at banks ATMs for cash, the Branch was keeping an eye on the situation. Likewise, during the implementation of newly introduced

Goods and Services Tax (GST), the Branch had to keep analyzing the new legislation from law and order perspective as it was a major tax related policy of the government affecting different categories of the citizenry. Then there are black-swan events, like a terrorist strike, the assassination of a VIP or a very serious crime like the Nirbhaya episode when the Branch has to really work very hard to collect intelligence so that the fall-out from such events is contained and does not go out of hand.

It may be understood that the quality of intelligence collection and the efficacy of the Special Branch depends on how much it has invested in creating and sustaining its intelligence assets and the processes it has in place. The work load of the Branch in the ordinary course of its business is so diverse and extensive that the system which has been put in place and tried over several decades stands up to deliver in such events even if the resources are stretched to its limits. Needless to say, like other organs of Delhi Police, technology is expected to play a major role in its work in the foreseeable future.

Special Branch of Delhi Police has been assigned the task not only of (i) collection, collation and prompt dissemination of Intelligence, but some allied functions like (ii) verification of passport applications; (iii) verification of character and antecedents of government servants' (iv) registration of Pakistani nationals visiting Delhi; and (v) issuance of Police Clearance Certificates.

Delhi Police personnel have internalized the fact that they are entrusted with the task of policing a city which is the seat of both the Union Government and the State Government. It is, therefore, a staging ground for all sorts of protest movements, demonstrations, rallies and dharnas by various organizations from different parts of the country and not just Delhi. The issues range from political, economic, social, to even international affairs. It also includes local issues of governance for which citizens want to agitate. But many of these issues are agitated in Delhi by protestors from other parts of the country as this is the seat of the Central Government. The issues may not be connected to the local administration or community and may be totally alien to the rank and file of Delhi Police. Even so, all officers who interact with the protestors have to develop an appreciation and understanding of the issues so as to take proactive action for the maintenance of order in the city. They should also be aware of the nuances of public mobilization. The Special Branch has to develop well-coordinated and verifiable advance intelligence but also maintain close liaison with neighbouring states, organizers of various events, organs of the police like local police, Traffic Police, PCR Unit and other government/non-government departments. This is accomplished through a series of coordination meetings at various levels. Special Branch invariably provides regular and timely actionable intelligence to all stakeholders through Special Reports, Advisories and Situation-Reports. It continuously monitors the situation on the ground till the conclusion of the event and even as a follow up in the aftermath of the event.

> *V.N. Chawla was an old Special Branch hand. In the latter part of his career he was posted as the SHO of a police station in the politically active New Delhi district, a hotbed of agitations and rallies .He performed admirably in this position solely on his intelligence background and the intimate knowledge of political organisations and their leaders .He always had advance knowledge of any demonstration and could defuse sticky situations thanks to his rapport with the leaders and the trust that they had ~~is~~ in him.*

In Delhi, Special Branch provides actionable inputs on all such events in order to help law enforcement agencies to take timely and proper decision. The activities of labour unions, student unions and religious groups are also closely monitored and timely intelligence inputs provided. Moreover, whenever there are visits of delegations from foreign countries it becomes imperative for Special Branch to analyze its likely impact on the law and order situation, as there could be some inimical groups in the city who may be opposed to the visit. A case in point is the visit of Chinese leaders against which the Tibetan exiles hold very emotional protests. High profile foreign dignitaries have to be given all possible security as the prestige of the nation is involved. Special Branch has to work in tandem with relevant Central agencies to provide timely intelligence inputs to various units to prevent any untoward incident.

COMMUNAL SITUATION

One important work of Special Branch is to keep a close watch on the communal situation, which essentially means, relationship between the different religious groups and its impact on the law and order situation in the city. From the pre-Independence era, maintenance of communal peace has been an area of challenge for the Indian police as even a small incident or a rumour can spark a major communal conflict. In fact, an incident anywhere in the country tends to spread to other parts of the country riding on rumours. The spread of electronic news media with its competitive emphasis on 'breaking news' and social media with its free-wheeling nature have added another dimension to the problem and has made the task of maintaining communal harmony even more complex. Special Branch has to keep upgrading its capabilities to keep pace with the changing technology of information dissemination. Consequently, it has had to wade into the cyber world to upgrade its intelligence collection machinery.

Apart from collection, analysis and dissemination of actionable Intelligence, the other allied tasks which fall in the domain of Special Branch, are enumerated below:

POLICE CLEARANCE CERTIFICATE (PCC) AND CHARACTER VERIFICATION REPORT (CVR)

Any private or public organization wants its employees to have a clean criminal record. For this they require police verification, or checking the person's police record which can have some authenticity. In Delhi Police, Special Branch issues Police Clearance Certificate (PCC) for the benefit of private organizations who hire individuals for various jobs. Many individuals also apply for foreign jobs where they have to mandatorily furnish a police report for emigration purpose through the Delhi Police website. Similarly, a Character Verification Report (CVR) is provided by Special Branch after background verification of newly recruited employees of government and Public Sector Undertakings.

Most of these services have become online with the use of modern digital technology and apps. The popularity of this service can be gauged by the fact that in 2019 nearly 1,94,702 applications for PCC and 32,146 cases of background verification of government employees, semi-government departments, public sector undertakings and private firms collaborating with semi-government undertakings were successfully handled by Special Branch.

PASSPORT VERIFICATION

Similarly, a police verification of any citizen who applies for an Indian passport is mandatory. The Special Branch plays a critical role in speedily verifying passport applications for citizens of Delhi. These are received from Passport Seva

Kendras located at several places in the city where passport seekers put in their applications. These applications are then sent to zonal offices of Special Branch for field enquiry. Passport applicants are informed through SMS service about the status of their applications, action to be taken and also the documents required for verification by the Enquiry Officer. During the year 2019, as many as 4,53,757 passport applications were received and disposed of.

PUBLIC SERVICE VEHICLE (PSV) VERIFICATION

The Special Branch is tasked to verify the owners, conductors and related employees including private employees of public service vehicles (like Delhi Metro, DTC, public buses, taxis, autos and e-Rickshaws). The idea is to ensure that persons using public transport should be safe and assured that the staff of such facilities is security cleared by Delhi Police. The potential criminal is also deterred from a criminal act knowing fully well that his record is with the police.

REGISTRATION OF PAKISTANI NATIONALS

The Special Branch is also tasked to register Pakistani nationals visiting India. It undertakes various tasks such as registration, long-term visa, exit and deportation of Pakistani nationals.

SPECIAL CELL

Terrorism is a relatively new phenomenon in India. It started in the 1980s with the Punjab problem. Till that time the Special Branch used to keep a watch over the activities of anti-social and anti-national groups operating in Delhi. But with the rise of extremism and terrorism, the need was felt for a specialized agency for collection of intelligence and counter-terrorist operations. Initially, a Cell was created within the Special

Branch for this purpose. In the year 1985, a Special Cell was carved out of the Special Branch and tasked to act as an independent anti-terrorist outfit for Delhi Police. It has now got an independent police station where criminal cases which are investigated by the Special Cell are registered.

The Special Cell is mandated to prevent, detect, and investigate cases mostly relating to terrorist activities. Nowadays, its ambit has been widened to cover other serious crimes, subversive activities, offences against the state, national security, public safety, Official Secrets Act, Explosive Substances Act, Fake Indian Currency Notes (FICN), narcotics/drugs traffickers, mafia/organized crime syndicates and interstate gangsters/rewarded criminals.

Intelligence collection and anti-terrorist operations undertaken by the Special Cell are based on human intelligence (HUMINT) and technical surveillance. The Cell has now increased its surveillance over cyber space as well. It also keeps a watch on radical ideologies, hate-speeches, inflammatory literature both physical and in cyber space. It also monitors and undertakes de-radicalization initiatives by analyzing the root cause of radicalization and the incentives of becoming a terrorist so as to come up with some effective solution to the problem. It undertakes ground level intelligence collection by checking hotels/guest houses and inter-state transporters at major *mandis*/markets. It also deploys sources to collect intelligence. The Special Cell has a technical unit to handle technical work like telephone and mobile phone monitoring, interception and cyber surveillance among others.

The Special Cell also has a Special Weapon and Tactical Team (SWAT) which was inducted into the Cell in 2009 to counter any armed attack and undertake hostage rescue operation. It has the capability of swift movement and undertake deployment for operations. It is capable of armed interventions in a terrorist attack like bus and Metro intervention, building intervention and other hostage situations.

The role of Special Cell of Delhi Police should not be underestimated. Delhi is a land locked territory and the city gets affected by the criminal activities in the neighbouring states. Similarly, with its proximity to the borders of the country, it also gets affected by terrorist activities. In such adverse geography, the Special Cell does a good work in keeping the city safe from such malevolent forces by developing intelligence and taking counter-measures. It goes to its credit that Delhi has not experienced any major terrorist attack in the last decade!

CHAPTER 7

The Specialists

Crime Branch, EOW and CyPAD

In the early days when life was simple and sedate, crime was also less complicated. Soon, the world of crime lost its innocence and simplicity. Criminals became wiser and started challenging the normal police efforts to curb them. This meant that the investigation work hitherto done by the police station had to become more specialized in order to handle the increasing complexity of crimes. These specialized police roles also had to move out of the confines of the station house. Consequently, a new breed of specialist investigators developed that shed the police uniform and became incognito by donning plain or civilian clothes. This specialized unit of detectives was initially christened the Criminal Investigation Department or CID. Further down the road, it came to be known as the Crime Branch.

The evolution of the Crime Branch is also reflected in the portrayal of policemen in Indian cinema. Till the 1980s a police person meant the uniformed variety. With the coming of terrorism and crime syndicates in cities especially Mumbai, many of the actions of the Crime Branch officers attracted wide media attention and like anything of popular culture, this entered the cinematic lexicon. The ubiquitous police inspector became the ACP of the Crime Branch. In parallel cinema, a simmering conflict between the two wings of the police was also sometimes apparent, with the Crime Branch shown as more elite than its uniformed counterpart.

Whether there is any rivalry between the two depends on the organizational culture and leadership of the two wings. But each has a chip on its shoulder. The uniformed police feel they are the repository of local knowledge of criminals. Being the visible arm of the force, it has the prestige and the wherewithal for law enforcement. Crime Branch personnel feel that they are the ones putting a lid on crime by quality and effective investigation, something which local police cannot, and does not, do. To me, this comparison is only the perception of those who do not appreciate the fact that Crime Branch and police station have separate mandates, and each has to carry them out without stepping on each other's toes.

At the end of the day the credibility of the police force depends on its ability to maintain order in society and specifically whether people feel safe. For maintaining the faith of people in law and order machinery, the role of the investigating agency is two-fold: prevention of crime and if it occurs, to detect the crime and arrest the criminals.

Prevention in the traditional policing system is ensured by the visibility of police through patrolling and general presence of policemen in the area. But with increasing sophistication of crime methodology and criminal modus operandi, mere presence is not enough. Police also need to keep an eye on potential law-breaking by collecting intelligence about local criminals and their activities. This is ensured both by technical means and by cultivating sources. In the present times when society demands a high level of accountability and transparency, police ensure that all the intelligence collection takes place within the boundaries of law and human rights so that their actions prove to be bonafide even if scrutinized at some later date.

If intelligence collection is proper, crimes are prevented even before actual harm is done. If the criminal is somehow able to give effect to his designs, it becomes imperative that they are apprehended and brought to justice as soon as possible. Once the criminal is arrested and sent to jail, this also acts as a means to prevent future crimes. This is because, firstly, the criminals are out of operation and secondly, criminals with similar modus operandi become aware that police is alert and keeping an eye. Needless to say, the Crime Branch is entrusted with both these functions: prevention and detection of big-ticket crimes.

CRIME BRANCH

The Crime Branch of Delhi Police is the primary unit dealing with anything connected with crime. With time it has achieved a high level of investigative competency and has been maintaining its standard in the field of crime detection, investigation and collection of criminal intelligence. The Branch earned the reputation of being a professional investigating agency and handled investigation of a large number of complicated and sensitive cases.

The success of the Crime Branch in catching criminals and ensuring justice is of utmost importance. It will not be an exaggeration to say that over the years the Branch has earned and retained the confidence of Delhi citizens by painstaking efforts to detect sensational crimes. In case of complicated and high visibility crimes, the leadership of Delhi Police turns to Crime Branch for immediate result in solving the case and minimizing the damage. For example, in numerous cases of 'kidnapping for ransom', the Crime Branch has swung into action to save innocent lives and prevent payment of ransom by the distressed family. In 2019, Commissioner of Police, had transferred 99 cases which were considered important for specialized and thorough investigation. During the same year, 45 cases were received from courts for further investigation. Even the Judiciary, aware of the investigative acumen of the Crime Branch, often assigns important cases to it. A hallmark of the abilities of Crime Branch is statistically evident in high percentage of worked out cases. In 2019, as many as 392 cases were solved with the arrest of 1500 criminals, which included 71 in murder/attempt to murder cases, 266 in dacoity/robbery/ auto-lifting, 158 drug trafficking and 254 white collar cases.

> *The Ministry of Home Affairs launched a sustained campaign titled* ***'Operation Smile'*** *in January 2015 throughout the country to rescue missing children.*
>
> *The Union Home Minister said that after the remarkable achievement, a similar campaign* ***'Operation Muskaan'*** *was rolled out in July 2015, and a total of 5679 children were rescued so far. India has ratified the United Nations Convention on Transnational Organized Crime (UNCTOC) and SAARC Convention to prevent trafficking of women and children.*

Strong professionalism has been the mainstay of the working of the Crime Branch. Astute follow-up of even the faintest clue in blind cases results in solving them. Crime Branch teams are also adept in solving gang- wars and shoot-outs on the basis of accurate information. Many of these sensational crimes are prevented even before they actually take place, saving lives and preventing further blood-shed.

Delhi's boundary is contiguous with two other states, Haryana and UP. Several other states are also in close vicinity. This makes it imperative that the Crime branch of Delhi Police, being the empowered agency for inter-state coordination, has to keep a close watch on the crime and criminals of other states as well. In the course of this monitoring, Crime Branch apprehends roving criminals from other states who are either planning a crime in Delhi or trying to hide after committing a crime in a neighbouring state taking advantage of big city anonymity. In either case, the Crime Branch has to do a very thorough fine-combing to achieve a measure of success in this game of blind-darts. It also extends support to other states in apprehending their criminals wanted in sensational and important cases.

For the residents of north Delhi's Swaroop Nagar, the automobile repair shop in their neighbourhood was no more than what it appeared to be—it was listed as such on services portals and on search engines as place to fix vehicle dents.

A Delhi Police team raided the shop, they found it was no repair store, but a place where stolen cars were brought and their registration/ chassis numbers changed.

The Delhi Police Crime Branch registered a case and arrested Sandeep Yadav, the car mechanic, while he was tampering with the chassis and registration numbers of a stolen Toyota Fortuner SUV.

According to an investigating officer, who did not wish to be named, an officer of the Crime Branch received information about an automobile repair store where stolen cars were kept.

Police suspect that Yadav and his accomplices, who have been active for the last three years, may have changed the chassis number of more than a hundred vehicles.

Accessed from
www.hindustantimes.com

The Crime Branch takes up the investigation of cases as complex as a criminal mind can conjure. On some days an inter-state illegal kidney sale-purchase racket is busted and on another a well-organized gun running racket is neutralized. Kidnapping for ransom, sensational murders, robberies, fake currency rackets, bank heists, espionage rings, illegal betting and human trafficking are issues that occupy Crime Branch officials over days and weeks, while they laboriously and tactically pursue slender leads to reach their targets. If you hear Delhi Police having worked out a sensational crime, in most cases, barring some terrorist-related ones or that of financial fraud, be assured that the Crime Branch has some role in it. Even in the other two, if this branch lays its hands on some actionable lead and there is the need for immediate action, it goes ahead to solve these cases as well. Every year Crime Branch arrests criminals carrying reward on their arrest, the reward money being shared by all the team members.

The above activities apart, Crime Branch is the nodal agency for dealing with the issues of human trafficking, fake Indian currency notes (FICN), drug trafficking, security of banks, wildlife trafficking, security of senior citizens, Interpol, etc. and is always facing new challenges in different fields. The Anti Human Trafficking Unit (AHTU) of Crime Branch investigates organized human trafficking cases and also undertakes special drives from time to time for tracing missing children under 'Operation Muskaan', a scheme of MHA. In 2019, a total of 626 children were rescued and restored to their families.

Crime Branch has various sub-units such as Dog Squad, State Crime Record Bureau, CRO, Public Relations Office, Research Cell, Senior Citizens Cell, Missing Person Squad and Finger-Print Bureau (FPB). These, as their names suggest, provide myriad assistance to police stations and other units of Delhi Police for the discharge of their various functions and responsibilities.

Finger-print personal identification is a distinctive discipline which has stood the test of time for more than a century in providing the most reliable and infallible scientific clue to identify a person. Apart from its utility in crime investigation, it is useful in identifying the owner of a property as finger-prints are generally affixed on important documents used to prove ownership. Fingerprints lifted from various articles found at a scene of crime help identify a suspect and link him to the crime. Earlier, the classification, storage and matching of fingerprints was done manually but now with the advent of technology these are done digitally. The Automatic Finger Print Identification System (AFPIS) installed in the Finger Print Bureau is connected with various remote query workstations installed at various police stations and units in Delhi. Besides maintenance and search of record, FPB also undertakes examination of questioned finger impressions on documents received from various investigation agencies, courts, State and Central government departments/ undertakings, etc. Experts of the Bureau also give evidence in the court of law and impart training in Finger Print Science to State/Central police personnel. Fingerprint experts are also posted in District Mobile Crime Teams to assist IOs in properly lifting fingerprints (chance prints) from scenes of crime.

Delhi Police has heavily invested in ensuring the comfort and sense of security of senior citizens. For this also, Crime Branch is the nodal agency and is actively associated with leading NGOs which are working for the welfare of senior citizens.

Several new initiatives in tune with the ethos of SMART policing have been taken by the State Crime Record Bureau (SCRB) being run by the Crime Branch. The SCRB is concerned with the innovative use of new technology and digital platform for law enforcement. Various apps have been created in order to simplify the processes of reporting and delivering police services by Delhi Police to the citizens of Delhi. In this also, the Crime Branch has a big role to play. They endeavour to identify newer areas for implementing technology and other innovations for improving police service delivery. For example, mobile and web applications have been developed to ensure online hassle-free registration of FIRs in vehicle thefts and other property theft cases. This not only ensures free registration of FIRs but prompt initiation of investigation into the complaints. The system also regularly informs the complainant of the progress of investigation. If the case remains undetected after a specified time period, the system automatically closes the case. The 'undetected case' is then seamlessly sent to a competent court enabling the complainant to file for insurance claim on timely receipt of the closure report.

Criminal intelligence being crucial to its operation, the Crime Branch is the nodal agency for the operation of Zonal Integrated Police Network (ZIPNet) and for implementation of the ambitious Crime and Criminal Tracking Network and Systems (CCTNS) project in Delhi. ZIPNet has data of crime, criminals, missing persons, unidentified dead bodies (UIDBs), stolen vehicles, etc. from eight neighbouring states, viz. Haryana, Rajasthan, UP, Punjab, Uttarakhand, Chandigarh, Himachal Pradesh and Delhi. It has been found quite useful by the investigating agencies of all the member states. The records of missing persons and UIDBs uploaded on the system help in identifying and tracing the victims. The ZIPNet database has been connected with motor vehicle theft application and e-challaning system. Traffic police is now connected with stolen vehicle database on ZIPNet and receives alert of stolen vehicles from ZIPNet whenever it is pulled over for any traffic offence on Delhi roads.

The CCTNS is a Mission Mode Project launched by the Ministry of Home Affairs, which aims at creating a comprehensive and integrated system for enhancing the efficiency and effectiveness of police. Its main plank is the creation of a nationwide network of IT-enabled state-of-the-art

With batchmates at PTC Phillaur, 1987 (Author seated second from right).

Author (in front) at the Passing out Parade at PTC Phillaur, March 1988.

Group photograph with the Governor of Punjab Dr. Siddhartha Shankar Ray & DGP Julio Rebeiro, 1988. (Author seated, first from left).

Author making farewell note at Gazetted Officers' Mess at PTC before the departure for Delhi, 1988.

Showing slum children how to mount a horse on their visit to Police Station Tughlak Road during Delhi Police week, 1991.

As ACP Chanakyapuri, 1990-94.

With staff and children at the Red fort on the eve of 50th Independence Day celebrations, 1997.

Author at a tree-plantation drive behind Red fort Delhi, 1998.

Celebrating birthday in the office, 1999.

Handing over the flag at a School Sports Meet.

At the Police post of Yamuna Pushta, Old Delhi.

Holding meeting with Chandni Chowk Ramlila organisers.

At a brainstorming session before a major law & order arrangement in North district (Author second from right).

Relaxing with colleagues (Author is on extreme right).

With members of Nagrik Suraksha Samiti in Old Delhi (Author is third from left).

Delivering the valedictory report at the Training Programme for Afghan Police officers, 2002.

At Pristina, during the assignment to UN Peacekeeping Mission in Kosovo, 2004.

With other UNMIK colleagues at Kosovo, 2005.

Group photo with the Home Minister, LG & CM after the award of Police Medal for Meritorious Service, 2005. (Author standing second row, fifth from left).

Author with a Pakistani police officer on a visit to Taxila, Pakistan 2005.

On VVIP security duty at Akshardham Temple, Delhi, 2006.

On a tree lined road in New Delhi as DCP Traffic, 2007. The iconic Ambassador official car is in the background.

At India Gate on the eve of Republic day 2014.

Author with a batchmate from Manipur during Mid Career Training at NPA, Hyderabad, 2014.

Giving a presentation before Commissioner of Police during his visit to PTC Jharoda Kalan, 2014.

Author receiving the President's Medal for Distinguished Service from Union Home Minister, 2015.

Awaiting arrival of the chief guest at the Passing out Parade at PTC, Jharoda Kalan, Delhi, 2016.

Author addressing a workshop held in collaboration with FICCI, 2019.

Author leading a patrolling party in the riot torn North East district amidst stone throwing and burning properties, February 2020.

Author interacting with rival groups during the North East Delhi riots, February 2020.

Taking a break with officers of Rapid Action Force during the North East Delhi riots, March 2020.

Author addressing probationers at Police Training College, Jharoda Kalan.

Author receiving the Prime Minister's Silver Cup from Union Home Minister at National Police Academy, 2019.

crime and criminal tracking system. CCTNS also provides for a citizen's interface to provide basic police services to citizens.

Another law enforcement unit which cut off its umbilical cord in this evolution of Delhi Police is the Economic Offences Wing (EOW). It was nested in the Crime Branch initially but as the number and complexity of white-collar crimes and financial frauds increased, there was a need that this category of crime, collectively called economic offences, required specialized handling. And so EOW came into being.

ECONOMIC OFFENCES WING

With increase in economic prosperity, financial frauds and white-collar crimes will gradually replace conventional property crimes in society. It would be a challenge for law enforcement agencies not only to keep investigating and prosecuting economic offenders but to constantly keep sharpening their own investigative skills to match the increasing criminal acumen. What makes investigation of economic offences challenging is the fact that its subject matter goes beyond the conventional training curriculum and the investigating skills required in a police officer. In order to be a good economic-offence investigator, he has to be an expert in financial and accounting concepts as well as in criminal laws and procedures. The number of cases registered and investigated by the EOW of Delhi Police in the recent years bears testimony to this increasing societal trend as well as immense faith in its investigative acumen.

Economic crimes cover a wide range of offences from financial frauds committed by individuals, companies and organizations, property frauds, share-market scams, job and investment rackets, housing and builders' frauds, bank frauds, multi-level marketing (MLM), Ponzi schemes and the whole gamut of Intellectual Property Rights (IPR) violations. All economic offences, one way or another, adversely affect the confidence of the public on the country's financial and monetary system. This willy-nilly creates a considerable negative impact on the progress of the entire economy and the nation, through the erosion of investors' confidence. In that sense, there is a lot riding on the EOW and the outcome of its investigation in complex cases. Invariably, the odds are stacked against it. Organized criminal racketeers and skilled professionals are often behind those offences drawn by the prospects of huge financial gains. Globalization, liberalization and market reforms coupled with advancement in ICTs and other technologies make investigation of economic offences very challenging. Added to this is the fact that each economic offence is unique and calls for a high degree of skill and professionalism amongst investigators for solving it.

In the year 1994 EOW was reorganized as a separate entity within the Crime Branch and with the notification of a separate police station in 2007, it started on its own journey. EOW is now a full-fledged specialized unit headed by a Special Commissioner of Police. An Addl CP takes handles the day to day operations. It comprises six sections each of which is headed by an Assistant Commissioner of Police. Two sections each are supervised by a Deputy Commissioner of Police. Economic Offence Wing as the premier investigative unit of Delhi Police is continuously striving to counter the growing complexity and number of economic offences through both, awareness programs for citizens and enhancing its own professional preparedness in prosecuting these offenders effectively and expeditiously.

The rapid rise in financial frauds of all types aided by the use of internet and computers has resulted in an increase in public complaints. EOW had to gradually increase its capacity. During the year 2019, EOW has handled 2189 complaints and investigated 1265 cases, besides arresting 192 persons involved in various economic offences. The impact of EOW's work on the incidence of economic offences depends on its ability to take concerted action against the perpetrators of such crimes. Being the nodal agency for economic crime investigation, it also provided technical assistance to the local police in investigating and apprehending the accused in various important cases.

With increasing complexities of economic offences and the proclivity of innocent citizens falling prey to the guiles of these unscrupulous elements who thrive on the ignorance of people, it is increasingly realized that citizens have to be made a partner in fighting this type of crime. With this objective in mind, EOW conducts various programmes to spread awareness about economic crimes and their prevention. EOW also release ads in important newspapers to make people aware about the common type of frauds. Very focused and targeted information is given to make people adopt common prudence and undertake due diligence before they make investments in financial or physical assets or enter into a business partnership.

In-house training programmes are also organized by EOW for investigation of economic offences wherein experts from various agencies including RBI, Banks, SEBI, NSE and other government/non-government organizations are invited for lectures/interactive sessions with twin objectives of capacity building and formulation of guidelines for public awareness.

CyPAD

For cyber offences which have registered a sharp increase in recent times, Delhi Police has a separate Centre called the CyPAD which stands for Cyber Crime Prevention Awareness & Detection Centre. This has been recently created as an independent unit. It is a specialized investigation unit for cyber-crimes like hacking, impersonation, online cheating, stalking and harassment etc. It is also the main unit entrusted with capacity building in cyber investigation. It is also a nodal agency for spreading awareness and for community outreach.

CyPAD has a state-of-the-art Cyber Laboratory to provide forensic assistance in cyber-crime cases. The laboratory is equipped with the latest software/hardware and knowhow for cyber forensics and cyber investigation. It also holds work-shops and training programmes for Delhi Police officers in investigating cyber offences.

A National Cyber Forensic Lab (NCFL), as a part of union Home Ministry's Cyber Crime Coordination Centre (i4C), has also been established in the CyPAD premises. This is designed to be a state-of-the-art facility covering all aspects of cyber-crime detection, retrieval of data, handling of various cyber forensic equipment, mobile forensic and the like. It will include cyber threat analytics, cyber-crime reporting & investigation, forensic tools, software & support, cyber research, innovation and training.

WAY FORWARD

There is not only an opportunity for all the specialized investigation units – Crime Branch, EOW and CyPAD to show their investigative prowess by solving difficult and sensational cases but to enhance the image of Delhi Police as a professional police force which is sensitive to the needs of the citizens and adaptive to changing requirements of the modern times. In this direction, these three important units of Delhi Police are constantly trying to bring about changes in their systems and processes and are totally focused on fulfilling the need of the citizens to find justice in serious cases, financial frauds and cyber-crimes.

CHAPTER 8

Straight and the Narrow

The Vigilance Branch

Police officers often complain that their work and conduct is constantly under public scrutiny. It is a fact that the police organization and the action of a policeman is being monitored constantly by the media, judiciary, legislature, statutory bodies like National Human Rights Commission (NHRC), Central Vigilance Commission (CVC), Anti-corruption Bureau as well as other oversight agencies. It is a common refrain that unlike any other government organization they work under very challenging and stressful conditions round the clock. The high incidence of suicide, alcoholism and depression among police officials is attributed to their stressful work environment.

Police service undoubtedly makes for a very challenging vocation. Any police person is called upon to perform duties under arduous conditions at the cost of their personal and family life. The work also involves a lot of risk both in terms of personal safety and occupational well-being. The duty hours are long and unpredictable. During festivals and holidays, they are at work, away from their families, doing their best to keep the city safe, and ensuring that everything is smooth and peaceful.

If it had only been the burden of long duty hours involving physical work, a policeman or woman would not have minded, even if they get only partially compensated for their long hours.

What disturbs them is the fact that there is very little recognition of their work and society at large is waiting for them to falter. They live under the prying eyes of citizens. Their actions are subjected to strict monitoring and any lapse attracts punitive action by oversight agencies, legislature, media, judiciary and even by their own organization. Their persecution complex is rounded off by their perception that even a bonafide action taken in the thick of battle is, subsequently, interpreted as an abuse of authority; even if the action under probe, helped in restoring law and order which they are duty-bound to protect.

There is a reason why police officers are under constant scrutiny by various agencies. The foremost reason is that they are the custodians of the law-and-order machinery. All their legitimate actions taken to ensure the maintenance of order have the backing of law. They can use force, search premises, seize property, arrest a person and ensure the attendance before them of any person—all with the force of law behind them. Police can also take *suo moto* cognizance of any offence. They have the powers to register complaints on the occurrence of an offence and investigate using the vast legal powers of investigation. If the law and order in a community is threatened, police can use force. While the law of the land bestows immense powers to police, it is natural it would demand accountability for its actions. And as a natural corollary it will impose certain checks and balances over its functioning.

In the present stage of evolution of governance in India, we have not yet reached a stage where one can say with confidence that there are no cases of high handedness or abuse of authority by police. It is not just a matter of interpreting adversely what the police perceive as their bona fide and mandated action. It should be kept in mind that in our country there is a vast majority of underprivileged people who are not able to enjoy their legitimate rights. In fact, most of them are not even aware of their rights. They are poor, uneducated and for decades have been denied their rightful place under the sun. No police officer worth his salt can claim that the action of police is always above board, especially in their interface with the vast majority of underprivileged people.

Without going into a taxonomy of allegations of abuse of police powers, some common ones made against the police are those of corruption, improper and tardy investigation, bias and prejudice against weaker sections, rude behaviour, human rights abuses and a general insensitivity towards the problem of the citizens. One major grievance of people is that police do not register their complaints. There may be a variety of motivations behind this refusal, viz. to project a favourable crime situation by minimizing the number of registered crimes, to reduce their work load, to show favour to some persons especially of the privileged classes or simply for reasons of corruption. There are also allegations of wrongful detention, use of third-degree methods and other abuse of power. Police are also often accused of using excessive force during protests or agitations. One of the frequent complaints against police is that of corruption. People have this deep-seated grievance that police officers extort money from people either to provide a service which they are duty bound to provide like registration of cases, release of seized property, granting of bail, etc. There are allegations of corruption also with regard to investigation where the case is deliberately weakened to favour the accused. Allegations of extortion from petty shopkeepers, hawkers, traffic offenders, to name just a few, are commonplace.

Since the police have so much power at their command, the possibility of abuse cannot be ruled out. In order to curb this, it is important to have a strict regime of oversight over their functioning. The best solution is to have an internal mechanism of monitoring the work of police through day to day supervision by higher ranks. This would ideally ensure that the police at the cutting-edge level adhere to the standards of work and conduct laid down for them. The responsibility of the supervisory levels would be to take effective preventive action and in case of any divergence from standards, to initiate immediate remedial measures. However, such an internal system of monitoring does not always function. This may be because of a reluctance to take punitive action against their own subordinates, as also a heavy workload of supervisory officers leaving little time for oversight. The limitations of an internal system point to the need for an external mechanism which can take prompt and just action on complaints of the public so as to restore their faith in the police system.

GRIEVANCE REDRESSAL MECHANISM

In Delhi Police, a separate Vigilance Branch is the main agency for handling complaints and ensuring redressal of public grievances. It is also responsible for issuing policy guidelines, coordinating with other bodies and monitoring of issues regarding redressal of public grievances. Although the Vigilance Branch is within Delhi Police, it is an independent entity with a separate chain of command directly under the Commissioner of Police. The latter takes the final call on all matters relating to vigilance policies, enquiries and follow-up action.

The Vigilance Branch is mandated to take necessary steps for redressal of public complaints, take necessary efforts to contain corruption and make working of Delhi Police more efficient and people-friendly. Lately, the stress has been on enlisting public co-operation to contain corruption. Its main objectives are: to strengthen public confidence in police, to identify and ensure corrective action against police personnel indulging in corruption or misconduct, protect innocent police personnel against false allegations of corruption and misconduct, and to liaise with other agencies in anti-corruption and vigilance matters. In addition, it advises on systemic changes impinging on public satisfaction with police services. The Vigilance Branch comprises the Vigilance Unit and the Disciplinary Action Cell. These units are supervised each by a Deputy Commissioner of Police both of whom work under the close supervision of Joint Commissioner of Police, Vigilance. While the Disciplinary Cell monitors the disciplinary and punitive aspects for timely and proper action against defaulters, the Vigilance Unit focuses on a preventive anti-corruption charter, apart from coordinating and strengthening the public grievance redressal mechanism of Delhi Police.

There are multiple channels for the public to lodge their complaints against the police:

Online portals: There are various online portals to enable the public to lodge their grievances quickly without any inconvenience, like CPGRAMS, PGMS & LG's Listening Post. While CPGRAMS is a web-based Centralized Public Grievance Redress and Monitoring System, designed and implemented by the Government of India, PGMS and Listening Post are maintained by the Government of NCT Delhi and the office of Delhi's LG. LG's Listening Post gives the citizens an option to register their grievances either on a toll-free telephone or on the website. It is handled on the Delhi Police side by the Vigilance Branch, which monitors the complaints after sending them to the Districts/Units for redressal. In 2019, as many as 13,819 grievances were received through this channel.

Other authorities: In addition to the channels mentioned above, complainants also submit their grievances to other authorities like NHRC, MHA, PMO, GNCT-CM Office, LG Office, CVC, PCA/PGC and various other commissions. The Vigilance Branch is the main agency coordinating with these authorities and for taking follow up action on each matter.

COMPLAINT MONITORING AND TRACKING SYSTEM (CMTS)

A citizen can now file an online complaint through the robust new system, CMTS. This is a unique digitized system designed for registering and monitoring all public complaints received in various units of Delhi Police. During the year 2019, a total of 96,142 complaints were received on CMTS, and taken up for enquiry. Special attention was paid to certain categories of complaints, such as corruption and extortion, land/property matters, economic offences, connivance of police in any organized unlawful activity and nexus with criminals, non-registration and minimization of offence, faulty investigation, misbehavior and physical abuse, dereliction of duty, etc., which have a direct bearing on the image of Delhi Police. The CMTS also enables Vigilance unit to undertake the analysis of various types of complaints so as to suggest proactive policy measures for correcting them.

CP'S POST BOX AND E-MAIL

Post Box No. 171 of the Commissioner of Police is a unique experiment which maintains the anonymity of the complainant. Each of these complaints is personally scrutinized by officers of the Vigilance Branch, and an impartial enquiry followed by expeditious action is ensured. Besides this, the email of the Commissioner of Police is an exclusive facility created for those members of public who may not be able to visit personally and yet wish to send their complaints from any part of the world.

In addition, public can contact offices of Delhi Police through various means to register their complaints, like telephone, officers' email, WhatsApp helpline and social media. Then there are designated helpline numbers like 112, 1091, 1093 and 1064, etc. on which complaints can be registered. A novel scheme of Public Facilitation Officers with inbuilt mechanism for obtaining feedback was introduced in 2017. It now covers 106 police stations. Moreover, in every district there is a Public Grievance Cell headed by an ACP. Delhi Police officers also have public hearings in which anyone can ventilate his grievance and the officers also get first-hand knowledge of the staff working under them. They can also conceal the identity of the complainant if they so wish.

The Vigilance Unit also exercises its function to check corruption through various innovative measures like:

Anti-Corruption Helpline: The helpline has the added advantage of receiving audio/video recordings, which can be used as evidence in support of the complaint. In the age of smart phones this is a very popular system of lodging complaints. Of late, the response from the public has been overwhelming. On this helpline, in the year 2017, 497 calls were received of which 283 were of police in action, 143 of corruption and the rest related to miscellaneous issues. These complaints were all enquired into with necessary follow-up action. This novel initiative has already gone a long way in sending a strong message to the police personnel of all ranks that corruption shall not be tolerated at any cost.

Flying Squad: The 24x7 Flying Squad of Vigilance Branch ensures prompt response to complaints of corruption or abuse of power lodged by citizens against any police person. In the Flying Squad, an officer of the rank of ACP, an inspector and other supporting officers remain available round-the-clock to raid and trap any police officer while taking bribes in real time. During the year 2019, 827 calls pertaining to allegations of harassment, inaction or corruption were attended to by the Flying Squad.

Special Surveillance Checks: The Special Surveillance Teams of the Vigilance Branch each headed by an Inspector rank officer, conducts surprise checks at various locations and traffic inter-sections in the city. The purpose is to keep an unobtrusive eye on those wings and personnel of Delhi Police such as Traffic Police, PCR vans and Police Stations which have a public interface to detect any instance of corruption while dealing with citizens. On detecting any suspicious transaction involving policemen on field duty, the Vigilance Branch officials promptly intercede to confront and take action against the policeman and any consenting member of the public.

During the year 2019, 257 police personnel of various ranks were awarded major punishments. 38 officers were dismissed from service. 1177 police personnel were awarded minor punishments. These actions followed enquiries conducted by the Vigilance Branch on public complaints against police misconduct or corruption.

Accessed from Delhi Police Report 2019

Surprise checks of Police Stations: Since the PS is at the cutting-edge of police functioning, it is an image hub where public perception and image of police is created or distorted. Keeping this in mind, the Vigilance Unit conducts surprise checks of various police stations to monitor the working of critical service-delivery systems such as Women's Help Desks, follow-up action on Dial 100 (PCR) calls, non-registration of FIR, behaviour with complainants, dealing with poor and

Delhi Police have time and again been criticized for not registering FIRs and for being rude and indifferent to the complainants.

To tackle this issue, the vigilance department of Delhi Police is sending decoy complainants to check the ground reality of police stations.

Cops pose as victims and visit police stations to check the conduct and response of police teams. From January to September 2017, as many as 344 decoy complainants have been sent to various police stations and in more than 10 percent cases, the police stations were found to be at fault.

Accessed from www.indiatoday.in/mail-today

weaker sections etc. Anomalies noticed during the checks are shortlisted for correction and improvement.

Integrity Monitoring: The Vigilance Unit maintains and reviews list of police officials with 'doubtful integrity'. Their names are placed in the list of personnel that have committed either a misdemeanour or an act of moral turpitude as per laid down standards of Delhi Police. In the year 2019, 528 police officials were added to the 'Doubtful Integrity' list.

EFFECTIVE COMPLAINT- REDRESSAL

Being at the top of the pyramid of public grievance mechanism of Delhi Police, the Vigilance Branch directly receives, handles and enquires into the public's complaints against police personnel. In order to ensure that even a complaint of a minor nature is well addressed and enquired into, it has established a system of public complaint resolution at various levels – Police HQ, Ranges, Districts and, Sub-division and Police Stations as well as various units. It keeps a close eye on the system by monitoring the progress and outcome of enquiries into complaints. Initially, all the complaints received directly or through other agencies are studied and analyzed. The unit then takes up the enquiry itself or assigns it to another agency at the appropriate level for enquiry. There is a set system of conducting an enquiry wherein all the allegations are looked at and an in-depth probe is made to unravel the truth. The complainant and the person complained against are also examined keeping in mind the tenets of natural justice.

Delhi Police places prime emphasis on redressing public grievances, and the Vigilance Branch acting as a nodal agency monitors complaints received through various channels. It facilitates their expeditious disposal. It also handles all important references from the Prime Minister's Office, the National Human Rights Commission, the Ministry of Home Affairs, the offices of the Lt. Governor and Chief Minister of Delhi, Public Grievances Commission, as well as from Supreme Court, High Court and Members of Parliament and several other statutory bodies.

System of e-FIRs in motor vehicle and minor theft cases to facilitate lodging of complaints. During 2019, the number of e-FIRs lodged were 2,33,191 (77%) out of 3,01,085 total IPC FIRs Citizens Services including grant of licence for casual performance shows provided on Delhi Police Portal. 1,05,66,445 Lost Reports lodged online so far, 10,03,645 citizens issued Police Clearance Certificate online, and 2,32,754 citizens issued Character Verification Reports online.

However robust the public grievance mechanism may be, it will only have limited utility if the basic functions of Police are not being properly carried out. The origin of vigilance complaints is in the upstream units of the police organization where people go with their problems but fail to get the right response. Therefore, it is imperative that all organs of the police organization and more so, those at the police-public interface work and deliver according to the legitimate expectations of citizens. Delhi Police is aware of this subtlety and has initiated necessary steps to monitor and manage this expectation gap. It analyzes the various categories of public complaints and recommends corrective action as well as policy reforms. Some examples of policy level initiatives to address critical issues generating public grievances are:

- Thrust on timely investigation and detection in heinous and sensitive cases (like rape and dowry related cases) through close monitoring.
- Expeditious arrest and charge-sheet of accused in offences against vulnerable sections and women.
- Appointment of Public Facilitation Officers in Police Stations.
- System of e-FIRs in motor vehicle and minor theft cases to facilitate easy filing of complaints.
- Online provision of citizen-centric services like grant of licenses, lodging of lost article reports, Police Clearance Certificates (PCC) and Character Verification Certificates (CVC) etc.

Therefore, it can be seen that Delhi Police is aware of the issues faced by citizens in its day to day interface with police offices at various levels. Rather than merely initiating punitive action against the defaulters, it is trying to solve fundamental issues which lie at the root of public grievance. One test of the success of such an endeavour and the ushering in of a new culture of policing in the country would be the steady reduction in the number of public complaints over time.

CHAPTER 9

The First Responders
PCR

Among the citizens of Delhi, Police Control Room (PCR) is the most visible wing of police. It is omnipresent in the form of hundreds of PCR vehicles stationed at different locations. It is easily recognized by citizens of Delhi, who not only acknowledge their significance but also rely on them heavily. It is also the most unrecognized and unappreciated unit although its role in maintaining order in this bustling metropolis is no less than that of any other wing of Delhi Police.

PCR has two important components: First, a Control room which is a call-centre located at the headquarters and second, a network of PCR vans connected to the control room and dispersed all over the city. Primarily the role of PCR is of a 'first responder' in an emergency. Any call on the emergency telephone number 100 is received at the Police Control Room, which directs the nearest PCR van to the spot. The PCR van upon reaching the spot takes an appropriate action as the first responder to an emergency call is supposed to do. But this simple process is carried out by a complex inter-play of man and machine.

For triggering the action of PCR in an emergency, any Delhi resident can call up the toll-free number 100 from the nearest phone. (The system is now shifting to one emergency number 112 for the entire country). The call lands in the Police Control

Room, where one of the *call receivers* picks up the call and quickly gets all the relevant details from the caller. The actionable information required by the PCR include 'what, when and where' of the incident being reported or any other relevant fact which the operator finds necessary to know. For example, if a crime is being reported, then questions may pertain to the type of weapon used, the identity of the victim and aggressor, whether the latter escaped or is still at the scene of crime etc. The idea is to keep the details brief but relevant to the point which enables the call receiver to categorize the emergency as low, medium or high priority. The emergency may not only be crime related, as people also give information of a fire incident, a power cut or even a monkey attack in the neighbourhood. This also speaks of the ubiquitous nature of PCR for the city of Delhi.

Immediately on receipt of the call, the call-receiver enters the information into his computer which is transmitted through a cyber highway in real-time to the *dispatcher,* who in turn, directs the nearest PCR van to the place of emergency. In case of any serious emergency, the call-receiver also picks up the hotline and informs all concerned officers and agencies like fire department, hospitals, and others just to make sure that there is no lapse or delay.

It goes without saying that the PCR operators manning the call centre are thoroughly trained and experienced to receive, categorize and relay the information further. At the same time, they are closely monitored by a supervisor who is located close by so as to give guidance in complicated and serious cases. All PCR personnel are deployed in shifts and so are the supervisors. Senior officers of the rank of ACP and inspector are present in the Control Room, round the clock.

There is never a dull moment in the call centre and the dispatch area of Police Control Room. Anyone who has visited an Air Traffic Controller (ATC) can find a similarity with the Delhi Police Control Room after seeing the frenetic pace of activity there. Pace apart, even the mandates of both are the same—to maintain order in their domain areas and save human lives. The utmost requirement for the personnel of both ATC and PCR is presence of mind and quick decision making.

> ***New Delhi:** At 4.45 p.m. on a Thursday, constable Anu's practised calm slips seconds after she picks up the phone and says, 'Namaskar ji, PCR channel Number1-2-0.'*
>
> *'Hello? Hello? He's beating my mother very badly, 'says the voice on the line, in Hindi. It's a young girl's voice, pitched high with fearful tension, sobbing between the words.*
>
> *Anu's voice wavers as she says, 'Where are you calling from? Who's hitting your mother?'*
>
> *'Please make it stop, 'the girl says, sobbing louder. 'My father is hitting her, there is so much blood.'*
>
> *'Tell me your location, tell me your location, 'Anu urges, barely suppressing her own panic.*
>
> ***
>
> *'We hear calls in our sleep, in our dreams,' Anu, who has been with the Call Centre for just over two weeks, says. 'Sometimes my family calls me on my mobile and I pick it up and say "Namaskar, PCR channel number" and they say, "Have you gone mad?"'*
>
> **Accessed from** www.livemint.com **dated 28 December 2017**

The Control Room is manned round the clock in three shifts. Each of the shifts has more than 50 operators manning the 50 channels for telephone No. 100 as well as some dedicated telephones lines for more specialized emergencies like 1091 (Women Helpline), 1094 (Missing Persons Helpline), 1291 (Senior Citizens' Helpline) and 1093 (North East People's Helpline). The call-receiver assigns the level of priority as High, Medium or Low, which is based on a standard protocol depending on the type of incident. Some designated crimes like murder, robbery, kidnapping, rioting, violence as well as crimes against women, etc. have been categorized as high priority. As soon as the priority level is keyed in to the computer system, other emergency services like ambulance service, hospitals, traffic police, local police station, district police control, fire service, NDRF (National Disaster Relief Force) are automatically notified and activated.

The call centre operators are monitored by an Inspector and his team constantly. They provide assistance to the call operators in case of any doubt or problem. For example, if the call is abruptly cut off or the caller is incoherent or seemed to be in distress, the operator takes the help of the Inspector, who can replay and listen to any call. All calls are recorded automatically when they are received in PCR. Very often this facility proves to be useful not only in responding to an emergency but in detection of crimes as the number can be traced back to the caller.

The Dispatch Room, located on another floor, is also a beehive of activity. It has operators called *Dispatchers* manning desks with computer monitors and wireless sets. The operators in this room are divided according to the PCR zones. Delhi has been divided into several zones for this purpose. The information entered in the computer by the call receiver in the floor below automatically lands on the computer of the dispatcher of the concerned zone depending on the area from which the call has been made. The dispatcher acts according to the priority assigned to it. For example, in a high priority call, he will bypass all other calls in the queue and transmit this information to the PCR van closest to the caller's location. He uses his judgement to select the *relatively free* PCR van depending on any previous calls they may be assigned to and still busy with. The aim is to ensure that a PCR van reaches the place of emergency quickly. This calls for alertness and presence of mind, especially in times of high traffic (in terms of number of calls).

It is very difficult to pinpoint which link in the PCR chain is more important than the others. The 900 plus PCR vans on the roads, including the 30 counter-terrorist 'Parakram' vehicles, are the visible face of PCR unit and in fact, the entire Delhi Police. Their work is without doubt very challenging. Some may call it interesting. When a call is received from the Control room on the computer tablet given to each PCR van, the staff, which is usually 3 or 4-persons strong, has to immediately move towards the place of emergency. On the way, they collect all the necessary details from the Control room on the radio or mobile phone. If needed, they also contact the person who has made the call. After getting all the details, they have to make a tactical plan on how to handle the emergency especially if it is not a routine call. And all this is done while they are on the move. Time is of the essence and their response time is being monitored at several levels.

The first challenge is to assess the gravity of the situation and the perceived threat to human life and property. They know that if the threat is continuing, it has to be neutralized first. The overriding priority is to save lives and reduce harm. The versatility of police first responder can be gauged from the variety of emergencies they handle. It can range from a terrorist threat, domestic violence, to fire in an apartment and from highway robbery to an accident victim lying on the road. The first responder has to move fast and remove the threat. In violent incidents, they have to neutralize the threat by using a range of actions from persuasion, verbal reprimand to the use of force, as per the intensity of the situation. On several occasions, they face imminent danger to their own personal safety. Such situations often make a hero of a common cop. Every policeman dreams of such an opportunity in his life time, but only a few get it. The acts of valour of policemen are often covered in the media and more often than not, these would be men from the PCR!

Delhi Police's PCR unit attended over 14 crore distress calls and took 37,527 injured persons to hospitals for immediate medical aid in 2019.

The Police Control Room (PCR) staff also apprehended 565 persons, including 72 robbers, 47 bootleggers and 111 snatchers, according to the statistics shared by the Delhi Police.

'The PCR vans support the local and traffic police in crime prevention and detection and law and order arrangements on a daily basis,' said a senior police officer.

'The PCR personnel have also acted as life savers in cases of drowning, fire incidents, and by giving CPR (Cardio Pulmonary Resuscitation) to victims,' he said.

Last year, live births took place in 14 cases inside the PCR vans while the mothers were on their way to the hospital.

In 04 cases, human lives were saved by the PCR staff by giving victims timely CPR who were struggling for breath.

Accessed from Delhi Police Report 2019

In ordinary course of duty, when the PCR van reaches the spot, and threat to life is neutralized or no longer present, the team leader who is generally a sub-inspector takes stock of the situation. He relays back to the control centre the full details at ground zero: type of incident, number of persons involved, weapons used and other relevant details. Many a times, the PCR van needs reinforcement specially while facing an armed gang or even a violent crowd. The PCR control then directs other PCR vans in the vicinity to come to its aid.

In case there is an offence of any kind, which is normally the case, the investigation officer from the local police station also reaches the spot with his team. Till the time they reach and take charge, the PCR van has to stay put in order to preserve the scene of crime and keep any suspect in its custody. Only after handing over to the local police can the PCR van go back to its base and that too after clearance from the Control Room.

If the PCR van finds an injured person on the spot, they do not wait for the ambulance but rush him to the nearest designated hospital, where another policeman from the local police station takes charge. The van is equipped for carrying an injured person and the staff is trained in some basic paramedic skills. Once too often, the PCR van especially in congested areas of the city also encounters problems in identifying the address. They are aware that the caller, especially in a stressful situation, gives an incomplete address to the control room or the operator may have recorded it wrongly. The calls made by the van are also not answered but still they are supposed to find it before any harm is caused to the person in distress. In case he is able to contact the caller, he may get some known landmark to reach the spot. Lately, the control room passes on the GPS location of the caller which helps in navigating it to the scene of crime.

The PCR also gets a lot of prank calls. They call them bogus calls. Such calls unnecessarily increase the work-load of the PCR. A call is declared 'bogus' only after the staff visits the given spot and have personally verified that no such incident has taken place. If they do it otherwise, it can cause embarrassment to all. Therefore, the PCR van keeps reporting the ground situation to the Command Centre. In case of a bogus call, the supervisory officer at the command centre calls up the number for a double-check. The reality of working in PCR is that they have to handle numerous bogus calls in a day. The proliferation of mobile phones has added to this problem. These do divert the PCR into an unnecessary drill but the PCR staff, both at the command centre and at the ground level, takes this as part of the game. But what is found unacceptable, especially by the young boys and girls manning the control centre, is the abuse and vulgar talk which some callers try to engage in. There are also bogus calls designed to spread panic like a bomb explosion or communal riots. Sometimes these are done deliberately with an ulterior motive, like an attempt to delay a flight or a train or the proceedings of a court. The caller knows very well that in case of a bomb-call the place has to be evacuated and sanitized. In such cases, the call is traced back to the caller and legal action is initiated against the pranksters.

The officer in-charge of the PCR shift keeps motivating and directing the staff to be quick in handling calls and to keep focus. There is a reason for this. A caller receives so many distress calls that it is very difficult for a normal human being, even for a cop, to remain totally detached and unaffected. Calls of serious accidents or deaths or the wailing of relatives does cause emotional stress. Similarly, any incident involving a child leaves a lasting impact on their psyche. But even before they can recover, they have another call to attend. The PCR control centre is always a buzz with the telephone rings. It is a subject matter of academic research how these calls affect the mental and emotional well-being of the call takers as well as the first responders of PCR.

There are peaks and troughs in PCR calls in a 12-hour shift, according to the activity level of the world outside. The staff have a fair idea of what type of calls to expect and when. The morning starts with calls regarding vehicle and house thefts discovered by people waking up from sleep. As the office time approaches, calls about traffic jams and road-rage take over. The most relaxed time of the 24-hour work-day is from 11 to 4 p.m. Again after 4 p.m., calls of traffic jams and road-rage re-appear. After 9 p.m. and throughout the night it is the time of drunken brawls, quarrels and understandably violent crime.

This is also the time for obscene calls targeting the women operators of PCR command room. They soon learn to ignore them and hang up. But outside these broad patterns, calls of crimes, fights, domestic violence and accidents keep the PCR staff busy.

The Delhi Police constabulary is mostly drawn from people outside Delhi, especially from the surrounding areas of UP, Haryana and Rajasthan. Lately, there has been an initiative to hold recruitment in all the states of India, a move aimed at making the force more cosmopolitan in outlook. This has posed a new challenge for PCR. The newly recruited personnel from outside the erstwhile recruiting areas of UP, Haryana and Rajasthan should be quickly acquainted with the geography of the city. Initially, they cannot make out the difference between Hauz Khas and Hauz Qazi, Kondli and Kundli. They also need to be familiar with the dialects and languages of the people. Failure to comprehend the name of place or the incident details can become a question of life and death.

Another very important requirement for someone to be deployed in PCR is to understand the life and cosmopolitan culture of Delhi. The PCR operators and other Delhi police personnel should not bring their own preferences and prejudices to interfere with their professional work, whether it is caste or community, or the way people live here. For example, an operator might receive a call from a drunken woman asking for help. This may be very unusual and generally frowned upon in a tradition bound hinterland of India. But the call receiver cannot allow his biases to colour his conversation and has to respond in a very objective manner. For many of these operators, a big city may look very queer where everything happens on 'fast forward mode'. He or she may find the patience and tolerance levels of the people here quite low. Even small quarrels between strangers can lead to a serious crime. Someone born and bred in the countryside may find this proclivity to violence and the inability of big city residents' to resolve even their small differences, very strange. But, the sooner they are able to accept the reality of this city the better it is for both the organization and themselves.

Apart from the mental and psychological frame of mind, a PCR person should have some language skills, which include English and even good Hindi. He cannot use the dialect he generally uses for his family affairs. This is true of most Delhi policemen but more so in PCR because his interaction with the citizen is in the context of a stressful situation. If people do not find their manner of speaking agreeable, empathetic, and soothing, it would only increase their stress level. This will also give a big dent to police image, which is generally formed based on the impression of the citizens about the police and their attitude at a time of crisis. Even if they do not have any bad intentions, the way they talk would turn out to be very important. It is very important that they lend a sympathetic ear to distraught citizens.

The need for training of PCR personnel cannot be overemphasized. It is needed not only at the time of induction in the unit but regularly in order to equip them with the broad spectrum of skills which they need for normal functioning. Actually, PCR personnel have to go through induction and refresher programmes which cover the entire gamut of necessary attributes like attitude, gender sensitivity, language skills, mental and psychological toughening to keep calm in stressful situations and similar skills in order to equip them to face the rigours of the job.

The term 'Total Football' was made popular by the Dutch team, a finalist at the FIFA World Cup of 1974. If there is one wing of Delhi Police which deserves to earn the prefix of 'Total', it is easily the Police Control Room (PCR). This is for the simple reason that the role of PCR is multi-faceted and multi-dimensional. PCR personnel have to be adept at nearly all the functions a police officer is trained and lives for. So far, we have only discussed the mechanics of PCR's role as a first responder. Even in the discharge of this role itself PCR policemen or policewomen have to display different facets of police role. They have to manage the traffic if they receive a traffic-related call. They take up this responsibility till the traffic police come on the scene and take charge. In serious traffic gridlocks they have to assist them in managing traffic. Likewise, when the PCR van responds to an emergency caused by an agitated assembly of people, they have to do crowd management. They generally start with talking to the agitators and try to cool the frayed tempers. This is a 'conflict management' role. However, if the situation gets out of hand and there is danger to life and property of citizens, they cannot wait for local police or reinforcements but intercede by using force in order to defuse and control the situation.

Similarly, in a terrorist attack the PCR staff has to face the first bullet. They have to try and neutralize the threat. Here, their counter-terrorism role comes into play. The PCR is also used extensively for security duties—both at the place of function and VIP route. Delhi being the seat of two governments, several levels of judiciary and numerous national and international institutions like Parliament, embassies etc. have enormous requirements for security of VIPs. Any Delhi Police personnel cannot be called a complete policeman unless he is familiar with security duties and has performed this duty at some point in his/her career. In that sense, PCR with frequent security duties provides a good exposure to its staff.

As mentioned earlier in the book, the most basic function of the police is prevention and detection of crime. The PCR is also called upon to perform this role when it is not responding to an emergency. The PCR van is stationed at strategic locations of the city. There are some iconic and sensitive areas like India Gate, Parliament, railway stations and bus stands, places of worship, etc. which are vulnerable to crime and terrorism and therefore need special attention. Then there are streets and areas of the city, especially those in proximity to schools, colleges and market places that are vulnerable to specific types of crime like harassment of women and children, robbery and snatching. Here also PCR vans are deployed as a visible presence of police and often end up detecting important crimes and criminals. They are also empowered to seize weapons, contraband and stolen goods. PCR vans are also given a fixed beat where they have to patrol at slow speed at different times broadcast by the Control Room daily. This increases the visibility of police. The patrolling and static duty times are changed every day based on an analysis of calls received from vulnerable areas. This imparts an element of surprise in the system. During checking hours, PCR vans stop and check suspicious vehicles and persons. They also have a list of suspect vehicles supplied to them by the PCR Control. This invariably includes stolen vehicles and those involved in crimes. The PCR vehicles manage to apprehend numerous such vehicles and criminals during their routine duties.

In fact, as a unit of Delhi Police, PCR has a long list of achievements including the arrest of some important terrorists. Readers may recall the Chittaranjan Park terrorist incident of the mid-1980s during the Navratra festival in which nine persons were killed and several others were injured. A PCR van acting on an alert by the Control Room managed to locate and kill one of the perpetrators when they had abandoned their motorcycles and had boarded a DTC bus. This is just to highlight the variety of activities that fill up a day in the life of a PCR cop, a point often missed in assessing their performance. Thus, those deployed in PCR have to be accomplished in several skills. Any wrong step in any of his assignments may lead to problems for him as well as the police department.

Another very significant but least known fact about PCR is that among all the units of Delhi Police, it is the first to adopt any state of the art technology. The PCR is heavily dependent on wireless technology to communicate with remotely located vans. It is also on a hotline with medical and ambulance services, fire brigade, local police stations, districts, neighbouring state police as well as other paramilitary and specialized agencies it works with. With Information Technology the bulk of its work is getting done through applications like Cyber Highway for sending instant message related to incidents to different entities for handling emergencies. On receipt of the call simultaneous messages are transmitted to four entities, viz. the nearest PCR van, police station, district control and in case of high priority incidents, the C4i, which is a specialized outfit. Each call is monitored through use of Information and Communication technologies, till its logical end. No call is left unattended or without any action taken upon it. The supervisory units keep pressing for an 'action taken' report.

Technology is also being used nowadays to communicate with the call maker. The details of the vehicle and its phone number are shared with him to facilitate direct interaction between them even before the PCR van reaches the spot. The PCR van staff is also given contact details and GPS location of the call maker to facilitate their navigation. For this purpose, they use a 'Phablet', which is used for making phone calls and also as a computer tablet to read messages, etc. Even in the backend, the PCR is using technology to improve its performance. They collect an online feedback from the public of various aspects of service provided to callers on telephone No.100. They have started using Big Data analytics to analyze the call pattern so that they can optimally deploy their resources. The wireless and other communication systems are also getting increasingly robust for ensuring better security. In the not so unforeseeable future, PCR would start deploying Artificial Intelligence and Machine Learning to accomplish its task and enhance its understanding of the requirements of citizens, thus improving its service delivery.

When the whole city sleeps, a citizen walking or driving on a desolate street in the dead of the night, can feel the reassuring presence of a PCR van, at a place where it is least expected to be. Ultimately, this feeling of reassurance is the greatest reward for PCR and its staff, despite the bullets and the brickbats it faces during the day.

CHAPTER 10

They also Serve Who Only Stand and Wait

The Support Units

The above line by the English poet John Milton from his poem 'On His Blindness' aptly describes the support staff of Delhi Police—the nuts and bolts, axle and shaft which work relentlessly and silently in order to keep the wheels of any police organization moving. They are invisible to the public eye but play a crucial role in delivery of police service. And if things go wrong as they sometimes do, they get more than their fair share of flak. While auditing the manpower in police, one can raise questions regarding the size of the support staff in comparison to the number of boots on the ground, which in modern jargon, is 'tail to tooth ratio'. But in analyzing their roles in granularity, one becomes aware of their indispensability to the organization.

There are full-fledged units like Communication, Motor Transport and Provision & Logistics, IT cell, Crime Record office (CRO) which give essential support to the front-line units at the cutting edge like the Police Station, Traffic police, Crime Branch, and the like. In addition, support staff is also present in every district and unit of Delhi Police. In the chapter on police station and its working, reference was made to the PS *Malkhana* and Record Room. These are also, in a way, internal support units which, along with several others, assist in the functioning of the police station. As already seen, an FIR cannot be registered, and investigation taken up or even a law and order situation handled without the crucial role of these support functions. Apart from the *Malkhana* and Record Room, there is a Computer Cell which keeps the IT system running and a communication person who keeps the wireless system in working order in every PS.

Mention has already been made of the Process Serving Unit at the police station, generally called the 5B staff. They are responsible for serving summons and warrants issued by the court during trial. Not serving the summons or warrants would further delay the court proceedings which are not in the interest of justice. This is a very sensitive task as any lapse would not go unnoticed by the courts already wary of huge pendency of cases.

Similarly, in every police station and district in Delhi there is a Dossier Cell which is responsible for preparing dossiers of accused persons arrested by the police. The idea is to build up the record of every criminal so that in future if he is involved in another crime which is not detected, the suspects can be identified by modus operandi, photographs and other biometric details in the database of the Dossier cell, which can help police in solving the crime.

One requirement of criminal justice system is for prosecution to prove the involvement of the suspects, beyond any unreasonable doubt, with the help of evidence. The main purpose of investigation is to collect such evidence so as to connect the criminal with the crime. For example, if a person is shot at and injured by someone due to enmity, the task of police investigation in crime team is to locate the weapon, the bullet fired from it and all other evidence to prove that the weapon not only belonged to the suspect but that he was present at the spot and had actually used the weapon to hurt the victim. This is a very simplified version of investigation. As can be gauged, police has to depend on its Crime team to support the investigators in collecting all the pieces of evidence from the spot and elsewhere. If the spot inspection and evidence collection is not done meticulously, important clues to detect the crime can be lost forever. Therefore, the role of the Crime team is very crucial in ensuring the delivery of justice.

The Crime team is a small group of forensically trained investigators adept in using equipment for identifying, locating and lifting clues from the scene of crime. A strand of textile fiber, hair, footprints, fingerprints, blood spots or anything can be crucial for connecting the criminal with the crime. All these have to be meticulously lifted, packed, labeled and handed over for safe storage. With increased emphasis on scientific investigation, the role of forensically trained crime team in police organizations all over the world has assumed centre-stage. In all serious crimes, a crime team reaches the spot along with the investigator. In earlier days, only physical evidence like blood and fluids, weapons and fingerprints were lifted by the investigators, which were then sent to the forensic labs for analysis and testing. The labs then gave their report to the investigator and also answered his queries on the scientific evidence, which enabled him to unravel the truth about the crime. The whole process was very conventional and straight forward. But now with increased use of IT and internet, the entire concept of evidence has undergone a sea-change. Now most of the evidence is in digital form and therefore the lifting of digital evidence has assumed a very important role. Consequently, the skill-set of the investigator has also changed with the requirements of technology and of law. Ultimately, any evidence is only as good as its usefulness in locating the criminal, and in prosecuting him in a court of law. Therefore, crime scene investigators, who are in the business of collecting evidence, have to be as good as the detectives if not better. The Delhi Police crime team members are aware of this fact.

Every unit or district in Delhi Police also has a clerical cadre called the ministerial staff for handling office work. There is a lot of paperwork and every reference or letter received from inside or outside the department has to be attended to, and action taken on it, as per existing procedures. The references received in a unit or district can be from the Police HQ, state or central government or any citizen. This has to be put up on a file by the ministerial staff, who are trained in office procedures and rules. The files travel up the hierarchy to the officer empowered to take decisions. Then it travels down the hierarchy, to the initiator for issuing the orders, as the case may be. All files, and there are multitudes of them, once they have been acted upon, are labeled and archived for the future. They are a rich source of data regarding previous decisions taken by officers. Old records are often taken out for checking if there is any past precedence. The clerical cadre is the custodian of this invaluable official record. When you do not get specific information about Delhi Police from any other source, the clerks can be trusted to ferret out the missing information. Even though the ministerial cadre is not supposed to do any core police duties of law enforcement, in crunch situations or in big police arrangements, as during Republic and Independence days, the ministerial staff is also pulled out from the offices and deployed.

There is a separate technical cadre to cater to the requirements of the force. They are as diverse as motor mechanics, electricians, plumbers and carpenters, as well as computer software and hardware experts. As and when required, expertise from the outside is also sourced. Every unit of Delhi Police has an in-house Motor Transport (MT) unit which maintains the transport fleet of the unit comprising buses, trucks, cars and two-wheelers. There are periodic inspections of vehicles by senior officers. Preventive maintenance of the fleet is regularly ensured since the rigours of the police job do not allow the luxury of extended periods of repair and maintenance. Also, the fact that a policeman is on duty round-the-clock makes the work of the MT staff all the more challenging. They have to get the broken vehicles back on the road as soon as possible. In case of major repairs, the unit-based MT section takes assistance of the parent MT unit which works under Provisioning and Logistics (P&L) department. There are also private vendors and authorized company workshops where the vehicles are sent for repair and maintenance.

The P&L unit itself, like its name suggests, is responsible for procuring and supplying all the articles needed in the police department–be it cars, furniture, uniforms or arms and ammunition. They go through a proper process of procurement to ensure the best available quality at reasonable price. The purchase or procurement process is done in the presence of various committees, members of which are senior officers from other wings of the police. Any unit which requires any high cost article can requisition it through the Police HQ which after approving it, sends it to P&L unit for its purchase and supply to the requisitioning unit.

P&L also has under its charge the Delhi Mounted Police, known as the Royal Mounted Police in the pre-independence era. The sight of a policeman on a majestic horse still inspires awe and fear among people. One can imagine it being used to suppress mass agitations during India's freedom struggle. But it was used for other purposes also and this is the reason why it continues to this day and age. Their use today is more ceremonial than practical. Although horses are no longer used for mobility but there are inaccessible areas like forests or thick foliage where they are still used in patrolling as no other means work. Mounted Police are also used during ceremonial parades to add a regal touch.

Prince (12) and King (15) are two of the Delhi Police's best stallions and were especially pressed into service after the force requisitioned the help of its Mounted Police to maintain order on Tuesday.

The Delhi Mounted Police have 50 horses (stallions and mares) and all of them were deployed in the city on Tuesday as the force geared up to deal with rising tempers in the city. The most experienced of the lot, black-coloured Prince and brown-coloured King were at work since 6 a.m. on Tuesday and worked tirelessly to ensure that the festival passed off peacefully. "Trained to work in riot-like situations these horses have been performing tricky tasks as and when required by the force," said a senior Delhi Police officer.

Sadly, King will be retiring next year as the stallion is now 15 years old and has to be put to pasture according to the rules of service. "King will retire next", year. During Muharram last year, he and Prince were on duty in the Old Delhi area, Divender, his handler said on Tuesday.

Adapted from www.dailypioneer.com dated 5 November 2014.

Even though this wing is no longer used for crowd management, it is an important part of police training. An officer's training is not complete unless he clears the riding test, which consists of mounting and riding a horse confidently in all its various gaits—trot, canter and gallop—and to undertake some basic jumps over obstacles and ditches. During our training we would question their relevance and were shut up by our instructors who told us that they were supposed to inculcate courage and confidence in cadets—attributes needed to develop into good officers.

In Delhi police, out of a sanctioned strength of 95 horses, there are only 25 horses at present. They are being looked after by 100-odd staff posted in the Mounted Police. The horses need a lot of care and attention from the staff, as they are prone to disease. They also have to undergo daily exercise and need proper hygienic diet. The Delhi Police mounts also win prizes in horse competitions like jumps and tent pegging.

Every time Delhi reports a heinous crime or is host to a VVIP event, Babu and Babe are the Delhi Police's most reliable investigators. Babu ,a five year-old Labrador Retriever, is the country's best tracking canine, while his sister Babe is among the best explosives detector canines in the country.

Babu had won the gold medal at the All India Police Duty Meet 2018 among tracking dogs while Babe grabbed the bronze medal in explosives detection. Babu's photograph was widely shared on social media after he took part in the 72nd Raising Day Parade of the Delhi Police last Saturday. "These two are the best we have. Babu's job is to track killers and suspects of heinous crimes while Babe is the best when it comes to tracing explosives and sanitising VIP areas before a major event.

***Accessed from* www.hindustantimes.com *dated* Feb 22, 2019**

Another member of the Delhi Police family is the Dog Squad. Beginning with their limited utility for infantry patrolling and for guarding, the roles of dogs have increased manifold in law enforcement in recent times. Endowed with a very strong olfactory sense, trained dogs are being extensively used as trackers in crime scenes, and as sniffers for narcotics and explosives. Presently, the police force at international borders and airports as well as other places deploy dogs for detecting narcotics. Similarly, with the advent of modern terrorism where explosives are widely used, explosive detector dogs have become a necessary appendage of counter terrorist units.

Presently, out of more than 200 breeds of dogs, 12 are used for army or police for their various purposes. In Delhi Police dog squad, presently there are 60 dogs of which 15 are trackers for crime detection and 45 are sniffers for explosives. These are mainly German Shepherds, Labradors, Retrievers and Doberman Pinschers. Any dog lover would testify about the high cost of maintaining a dog. They need proper diet, regular grooming and constant veterinary care. Police dogs need even greater care as they perform long and arduous duties most of which are outdoors. They are very susceptible to serious diseases due to constant sniffing of chemicals present in narcotics and explosives. Since the police breeds are of foreign origin, they are also very susceptible to the extreme climatic conditions in Delhi. They are especially sensitive to the city's summer heat. Therefore, dogs are kept in air-cooled environment. A veterinarian is also available to take care of the dogs. It may be mentioned that sniffer dogs are trained nearly every day by exposure to prohibited and contraband substances like narcotics and explosives. Wherever any new substance comes to the notice of Intelligence Agencies, the sniffer dogs begin training to identify these as well.

Coming back to the core function of crime prevention and detection, there is one support unit—Crime Record office (CRO)—which gives invaluable inputs to all the investigation units. Armed with statistics of every case registered by the 140-odd police stations in Delhi, the unit analyzes the underlying crime patterns and assesses effectiveness of various initiatives for reducing crime. Their inputs help in giving shape to crime prevention strategy of Delhi Police. The CRO works under the Crime Branch and is forever trying to improve its analytical power by use of IT and data analytics. Now, there are plans to start using Data Analytics and Artificial Intelligence (AI) to unravel hidden patterns in crime statistics, predict crimes and to identify the suspect and accused.

Last but not the least, Delhi Police is served by a cadre of essential but invisible men and women called the MTS or Multi-Tasking Staff. These are cooks who prepare healthy meals for the thousands of men and women who eat in the police mess. There are sweepers and other house-keeping staff to keep the police premises neat and clean. Then there are the gardeners, water-carriers and other tradesmen like cobblers, washermen, carpenters and plumbers. Inconspicuously and silently, they go about their work to keep the police system working smoothly, day after day, year after year.

CHAPTER 11

Blow Hot, Blow Cold

Relation with Citizens

The citizens of Delhi have a very complex relationship with their city's police. One day they thank the police for taking prompt action in a case and the very next day they block roads on some other issue demanding action against them. On one day praise will be heaped on them for a serious case solved and the day after complaint will be filed against them for not recovering their property in the same case. The police, on the other hand, believe they work long hours, take heavy personal risks but everything comes to naught by the grumblings of an ungrateful populace. They often feel that the people are unforgiving even for small and genuine errors committed in the discharge of their duties.

Delhi Police's relationship with the citizens has been crafted by destiny and conditioned by history, culture and geography of the place. The mutual perception of the two opposite sides, who are actually stakeholders, point not just to a complex relationship but to high expectations which sometimes do not get fulfilled. In the age of anomie, police very often are the only conscience keeper for citizens. If they have an issue with their neighbour, the local shopkeeper or even a civic agency, they run to the police, regardless of the fact that the matter may be minor or 'civil' in nature, where no police action is warranted. When the citizen knocks the door of the police, what they expect is sensitivity and politeness. If the policeman behaves rudely or brusquely, this experience leaves an indelible mark on their psyche.

When grievances of citizens against the police pile up, these might in part trigger a broader protest, which Delhi Police has had to face at various times. However, it can be mentioned to the credit of Delhi citizens that even at the lowest ebb of its relationship with the police, they do not allow their prejudices to affect their rapport with individual officers. A personal experience of the early 1990s can be narrated when this writer was invited to a wedding at an ITDC hotel. The staff who were at the receiving end of a police action the previous day were present in large numbers. They were part of a group demonstrating against the privatization of their public sector company. When the gathering had started indulging in violence, I had to order the police to disperse them. Tear-gas and mild force were used as per the standard operating procedure. Since I was identified as the officer who had ordered the use of force on the congregation, it was natural for them to express their ire against me. But that evening, contrary to my apprehensions, they were very sporting and only joked about the said incident. I was touched by this as, on the previous day, tempers were running really high and they had been complaining vehemently against police action. This incident changed my entire perspective of police-citizen relationship. I should add that nothing different has happened subsequently to change this impression in anyway.

In order to understand the relationship between police and citizens, we must see the various points of contact between the two. The first and the most basic interface is when a citizen approaches the police with a complaint. This can relate to some harm caused by one person to another whether on body, property or reputation. The complaint can also be against the action of a government functionary or an institution, including police. If a cognizable offence is made out, the police are obliged to register a case. If the offence is doubtful, the complaint merits an enquiry.

The basic contact of public and police causes friction and often leads to grievances on both sides. The public feel that their complaints are not being attended to in right earnest. The police do not register an FIR to start investigation even though, in their view, a clear criminal case is made out. Even if an enquiry is taken up, often the people have the grouse that it is not being done the right way and that the findings will not be fair and proper; that the effort of the police has been to either trivialize or disprove the allegations of the citizens. Soon complaints of corruption, of having taken a bribe from the opposite party, are levied. Police are also blamed for brushing the complaint under the carpet, especially if the allegation is against police personnel.

The police, on the other hand, feel that people file false complaints against their rivals and enemies to settle scores; that they often exaggerate an incident to make it seem serious so as to hoodwink the police to register an FIR in order to have an upper hand against their adversary. In the same vein, the police feel that they file false complaints against policemen to pressurize them to act according to their whims and fancies. In my view, there are unscrupulous elements on both sides—complainants and also policemen, so a sweeping generalization is rather unfair. It is the duty of police to get to the bottom of an issue and after digging out the truth, act in a fair and fearless manner.

Similarly, it is the responsibility of citizens to resist the temptation of filing false complaints against someone to get even with him. The institution of police should not be misused by anyone to settles cores as ultimately it will harm society in the long run. Police being the custodian of law and order in society should be encouraged and supported to be fair and objective in their dealings. The tendency to exaggerate or minimize the offence by both the parties—police and citizen—should also be discouraged. It is also expected from a responsible citizen that he or she intervenes for settling minor issues within the community to avoid unnecessary complaints. A responsible and mature citizenry deserves a trusted and professional police force. Maturity is what is expected from both citizens and police so as to avoid unnecessary conflict and therefore, wastage of time and energy. This would also reduce the stress level in society and usher in a truly welfare state. However, being a disciplined outfit Police have to show more tact, patience and professionalism in its dealings.

Another point of contact with police is when the citizens approach them for any service which only police can offer. Applying for a Police clearance in order to obtain a passport is one such occasion. The concerned department of the government issues a passport to a citizen of India only when they receive his police record. The latter look up the criminal record based on the place of residence of the applicant. They also refer to their criminal database. Similarly, a citizen needs a Police Clearance Certificate (PCC) for many other purposes, one of which is to apply for a visa or permanent residency of a foreign country. Citizens also need PCC while applying for a job or if they are employing someone. Police also conduct an antecedent verification of tenants, as well as employees like servants or guards hired by a citizen.

In providing all these facilities, police have a monopoly as they are the sole custodian of crime data. But, despite its monopoly, police cannot afford to reduce their level of service. In fact, Delhi Police is aware of the fact that service delivery of this kind can earn them a lot of brownie points. In a sense, this is a kind of positive role of the police. On the other hand, law

With the aim to further strengthen good governance practices in the working of police, Ministry of Home Affairs has commissioned the Bureau of Police Research and Development to conduct a pan-India survey called "ALL INDIA CITIZENS SURVEY OF POLICE SERVICES". The survey will be conducted through the National Council of Applied Economic Research, New Delhi.

Accessed from http://pib.nic.in/newsite/PrintRelease *dated 21 February 2019*

enforcement which is the core area of policing necessitates penal and even physical action at certain times. These are perceived to be negative roles by society. For this reason police is always trying to improve the service delivery in areas like passport verification, issue of PCC, licensing, and so on, which are not related to law enforcement functions.

A plethora of digital initiatives like online registration of FIRs, NCR, passport verification, online application for PCC and others have been introduced in recent years. The objective is to bring Delhi police to the doorstep of every citizen, and there is no better way to do this than by the digital route.

Another service which is available to the citizens of Delhi is the grant of license for various purposes. The most common is the license to own or carry weapons in the city. A citizen needs weapons for various purposes – like security, sports and even hobby. Sometimes, they do not want to part with a weapon which is a family heirloom. For any of the above reasons, residents of Delhi have to apply for an Arms License and only if it is granted by the police, they can possess, keep or carry a weapon and the ammunition. The important criteria for obtaining a license are the applicant's clean criminal record and the genuineness of his or her need.

A citizen also needs licenses for pursuing certain vocations like owning and running a restaurant, a hotel, press or publication, petrol pumps, explosive dealerships, cinema hall, discotheque to name some important ones. Institutions like hotels, schools and clubs also require a separate license for swimming pools and auditoriums. Licenses are also required for casual performances like dance shows, plays and films. The idea of having a license is not to constrain the citizens' freedom but to ensure that certain standards for public safety, security and convenience are followed and law & order is not disturbed in the city.

> ***Old Guard: Delhi Police's Senior Citizen Cell does more than just dropping by homes of the elderly***
> *A doctor's appointment, a row with neighbours, a lost key—the Delhi Police's Senior Citizen Cell does more than just dropping by homes of the elderly.* The Indian Express *travels with beat officers to homes of men and women above 60 to explore the various relationships they have forged.*
>
> *Accessed from indianexpress.com dated 25 June 2019.*

For Delhi Police this is a huge responsibility and also an opportunity to leverage it for establishing closer ties with the people of the city. This is an important point and needs some elaboration. The role of police in society is generally negative, as it symbolizes the enforcement and maintenance of law & order. Both, in the process of preventing an offence and detecting a crime, the invocation of legal and penal provisions becomes necessary, which can be construed as coercive. But grant of a license is invariably viewed as something positive and this annuls to some extent the negative aspect of policing.

All police forces in the country do not have licensing powers. From the colonial days this power has been exercised by the District Magistrate. But the introduction of Police Commissioner System in 1978 gave these powers to Delhi Police Commissioner. A lot of initiatives have been taken to streamline the process of issuing various licenses. Initially, in the pre-computer days, new systems and processes were set up. Nowadays there is an emphasis on applying modern management principles including Information Technology to ease the process of grant and renewal of licenses. A balance is maintained between the requirements of rigorous verification and ease of doing business so that licenses are not granted to undeserving parties. Delhi Police is conscious of the fact that in the present age of online transaction and home delivery of merchandise, the expectation level of people is very high. Not that the public do not want due verification but what they do not want is harassment or the prying *Inspector Raj* in their dealings with the government. If any government agency falters, the vocal and aware citizens whose number is steadily increasing do not hesitate to air their grievance online, through social media or physically, through visits and phone calls to senior functionaries.

Delhi Police is consciously taking efforts to not only streamline its service delivery processes but also improve its grievance redressal mechanism across all departments. Police officers and men are also continuously imparted customer-sensitivity training so that they are aware of the requirements of the changing times. If, after all these organizational endeavours, the police officers do not change their attitude and ways of working, then punitive mechanism comes into play. The incorrigible employees are banished to non-sensitive units where there is minimal contact with citizens.

One area where police have grievance against the citizens is reporting of crimes. Police feel that citizens have to honestly discharge their basic duty with regard to sharing information about crimes, criminals and anything which has the potential to create disturbances. The police say that even if there is a day-light incident, people prefer to be bystanders. As soon as they are requested to speak about the incident, the crowd just melts away. No one is willing to stick his or her neck out. On the other hand, people argue that they will get into the unnecessary hassle of visiting police stations and subsequently getting summoned by courts for recording their evidence. They are also wary of creating enmity with criminals.

This problem has been highlighted in Indian cinema quite emphatically. The reluctance of the people to report crimes and stand as a witness is generally portrayed as a typical response to a reign of terror unleashed by lumpen elements acting at the behest of a local political--business–police nexus. In real life such a criminal collaboration is rare if not improbable. But the fear gets imprinted in the minds of ordinary citizens making them mute witnesses to crime. They are reluctant to come forward and testify due to fear of reprisals at the hands of criminals. This really restricts the police. When the criminal trial begins, the first question police are asked there is no 'independent public witness' since the crime was committed in broad daylight or in a public place. The credibility of such independent witnesses is high. All other witnesses like the victim's relatives are treated as 'interested' witnesses that have a lower credibility.

The police find themselves in the same category of being 'interested'. A common refrain among policemen is that at the time of trial they stand alone, trying to get the accused prosecuted. All around them is an air of suspicion that an innocent person has been wrongly arrested by the police in order to solve a crime.

But to be fair, there is some basis for the reluctance of the general public to go to the court in support of police. They do face a lot of inconvenience. For instance, they have to take leave from work and often the case gets adjourned. They are then summoned on another day. Cases are frequently adjourned on one pretext or the other like absence of the accused, lawyer or even the judge. Although police is not blamed for this harassment, it does affect their work. The introduction of technology in a big way, like examination of a witness or accused from remote locations and other measures would reduce the problems of adjournment and delays in court proceedings. This has been widely used by all courts during the recent corona-virus pandemic and the system has adapted itself quite well. If it is made a regular feature, it would go a long way in addressing the grievance of the people.

In recent days, there is a very strong emphasis in making government departments including police more accountable, open and responsive to the needs of the public. Information technology-based services like interactive websites, apps and social media are widely used. Government departments are also streamlining their processes and simplifying the rules. Delhi Police has also taken several steps in this direction and gradually the values of responsive public service and sensitivity to the citizens' needs are getting instilled in the rank and file of police.

There are initiatives by citizens of Delhi also to bridge the gap between them and the police. There are NGOs and civil society organizations which conduct various programmes for mutual appreciation of challenges and expectations between police and citizens. There are outreach programmes that highlight the achievements of the police. Some of them also hold workshops for police personnel to make them more sensitive and responsive to the problems of the citizens.

Then there are groups of civic-minded citizens that work with police for improving law and order, in community policing initiatives by several police forces in the country, including Delhi Police. There are volunteers doing traffic management duties, in normal times as well as during festivals, fairs, processions, and so on. Groups of conscious citizens perform patrolling duties along with the police, especially during night hours. There are various schemes of community policing in which the community members organize themselves for setting goals for law enforcement and undertake general crime prevention and other policing duties. The 'Neighbourhood Watch Scheme' (NWS) is very popular in several colonies of Delhi. Under NWS, civic-minded community members are mobilized in order to assist the police in law enforcement by holding workshops, bringing out pamphlets and brochures outlining basic precautions to be taken by citizens and assisting in patrolling and other law enforcement duties in the area.

Many of these initiatives help in changing the attitude of people towards the police. This is, however, going to be a very gradual process and requires sustained efforts in that direction. Age-old prejudices reinforced by headline-grabbing media reports on police excesses, cannot disappear overnight. But with the use of technology and by setting up improved systems and processes for ensuring accountability and transparency, a positive change in public perception can ensue. Similarly, changes in other organs of the criminal justice system, ensuring speedy trial, would slowly reduce reluctance on the part of people to work with police in reporting and fighting crime.

Even at present, citizens can ensure that Delhi Police is accountable and transparent in its working. This is by being more proactive and participative in matters concerning law enforcement and police. Senior officers are mandated to fix a time for listening to the grievances of the public. Action is taken immediately on receipt of a complaint or after hearing the complainant in person. Then there are units like the Vigilance Branch that works directly under the Commissioner of Police. In addition, all the field units like police districts have an ACP in-charge of the Public Grievances Cell (PGC) and he reports directly to the DCP of the district/unit.

Citizens can also elicit information from the police through an application under Right to Information (RTI) Act. The police are obliged to provide all information connected with the applicant even if they pertain to more than one district or unit. The RTI is a very effective means of empowering the people through removing the information asymmetry.

Police is wary, however, of certain unscrupulous elements that use the police to settle their personal scores. They take advantage of the facility to lodge an FIR based on an exaggerated or even a false complaint. On the other hand, there are some unscrupulous elements in the police who, although in minority, have still not imbibed the values and virtues of a professional and sensitive police force, who do not hesitate to harass the public for their own ego and narrow self-interest. The true worth of police, thankfully, can be discerned by an aware citizenry. Delhi Police is waiting for that day when its true character blossoms and its commitment to making Delhi a more livable place is fulfilled.

CHAPTER 12

The Times They are a Changin'

Technology, Smart Policing and the Way Forward

Police have been one of the early adopters of technology in India. Beginning with the introduction of bicycles and motorcycles for replacing foot patrol and horses to the use of personnel carriers and helicopters, the need for rapid mobility has been the main driver for change. Soon in other operational areas like communication, weaponry, crowd control, traffic management and later, counter-terrorism use of technology gave police an edge. In the present time, myriad facets of law enforcement are being adopted for state-of-the-art technology like Data Analytics, Robotics and Artificial Intelligence. At the same time, Information Technology (IT) is being increasingly used for various police work including internal administration, financial and manpower management as well as for reaching out to citizens.

From time immemorial, human beings have felt the need to communicate messages to far-off places. In the older days, they conveyed messages by runners as messengers. They also used smoke signals and beating of drums which could be relayed from one village to the next till it reached the intended recipient. Anecdotally, pigeons were also used, with messages tied to their feet or around their necks. With the coming of technology, Morse codes were used to transmit signals with some degree of secrecy and speed. The telephone gave a big fillip to how humans communicated up until then. Even though telephones enabled two-way real-time voice communication, it had its limitations in terms of cost since cables had to be laid from point to point.

Wireless telegraphy was the game changer. Its invention not only changed the way we communicated but laid a solid foundation for further advancement in communication technology. It also came as a big boon for the armed forces and the police as it served the purpose of both speed and secrecy. As the name suggests, wireless system enables flow of information between two or more points where there is no wire or cable between the sender and the receiver. The most common wireless technology uses radio waves. Among police forces in India, Delhi Police was one of the early adopters. Beginning with wireless radios at selected field locations like police stations, Delhi now has a very sophisticated and secure wireless system covering various establishments. These include fixed wireless sets at police stations, districts and PCRs, mobile sets in all police vehicles and portable systems for officers and men in the field. Communication is secure and real-time with little disturbance. The signals are also encrypted, which ensures no intruder is able to snoop into the communication. These days, mobile phones are also frequently used for communicating but policemen generally avoid it for confidential communication due to security concerns.

Apart from communication and mobility, nowadays technology, especially Information and Communication Technology (ICT) is commonly used to leverage the performance of police in its core areas of functioning. ICT is the back bone of the Crime and Criminal Tracking Networks and

Systems (CCTNS), which enables storage, retrieval and analysis of crime and criminal data—widely used for crime investigation. ICT backed with sensors is also the basis for Area Traffic Control (ATC) system-an important traffic management innovation. In this, real time traffic data is transmitted to a central computer which then determines the signal timing at remote traffic junctions so as to optimize the traffic flow in the entire road network.

In a city like Delhi, police also rely a lot on CCTV cameras which serve as additional eyes of the police. Numerous cases are solved with the help of these cameras which capture the image of unsuspecting criminals. ICTs are also used for digital data communication between offices and officers. Similarly, for internal office administration also, especially for manpower management, and financial functions, computers are widely used. These days proficiency in computer use is an important prerequisite for recruitment even at the constable level.

ICTs and internet are widely used to reach out to the public. User-friendly websites of Delhi Police with separate pages for important units have been created for dissemination of information to the public. Also, on-line complaints can be filed in certain cases like in cases of theft of vehicles, cybercrimes and the like. The procedure of filing of a police report in matters that are non-cognizable which means police cannot start investigation without a court's order, has been simplified. These reports called the Non-cognizable Report (NCR) for issues like loss of one's documents and other articles can be done online. Citizens need the NCR in order to file for a duplicate document or to claim insurance but had to run from pillar to post to get them from their police station. Several Apps have also been developed and launched by Delhi Police. For example, the 'Himmat Plus' app is for seeking emergency police response on the apprehension of any harassment or threat to a woman. More and more apps are being developed for bringing police service closer to the people. Delhi Police is constantly using IT by leveraging the increased use of smart phones and the spread of computer literacy among citizens.

There is a flipside to modern technology. Its easy availability, low cost and user-friendly nature has made criminals quite tech-savvy. They use modern technology-whether embodied in mobile phones, wireless systems, computers or weaponry—to add new challenges for law enforcement. However, the same technology is helpful to the police. Law enforcement agencies all over the world solve a lot of cases by analyzing the digital footprints of a suspect using his computer, social media and mobile phone records. A continuous cat and mouse game goes on between police and criminals to upstage each other in the use of technology.

Another area of technology which has wide application in the armed forces and police is weaponry. Traditionally, officers in Delhi Police from the rank of ASI upwards carry a small weapon whereas the constabulary carries long range weapons. The carrying of arms by officers is common for law and order and VIP security duties. Police officers on the beat did not generally carry weapons except cane sticks. But, after the advent of terrorism in the 1980s, it has become imperative for officers on other duties also to carry arms.

There has been rapid technological advancement in the area of weaponry — leading to design of weapons with more effective fire-power and better 'ease of handling'. In small weapons, initially revolvers were generally used. These were of 0.45 calibre and later on of 0.38 or 0.32 bore. Subsequently, 9 mm pistols replaced the revolvers. Nowadays, Glock pistols are in use. In long range weapons, in earlier times, muskets were used. But after independence, these were replaced by 0.303 Lee-Enfield rifles. Although not very easy to handle, the 0.303 had a very accurate fire-power. The need for quick handling and use brought in the automatic weapons like SAF Carbines and Sten guns. AK-47 and MP5 weapons have now replaced the carbines.

SMART POLICING

Smart policing is the new buzz word. It was formally included in the police lexicon in India when the concept was first proposed in 2014 by none other than the Indian Prime Minister. SMART was initially used as an acronym for *Strict and Sensitive, Modern and Mobile, Alert and Accountable, Reliable and Responsive, Techno – savvy and Trained*. This way of defining smart policing makes it more comprehensible for the common man. However, 'smartness' implies much more than the attributes the acronym refers to. Smart policing is a more comprehensive and durable concept. It is basically good policing. Any contemporary police force can be called *smart* if it is intelligent enough to solve the emergent problems of the people in the most effective way by applying modern tools and techniques and at the same time observing the canons of a

> *Prime Minister, Narendra Modi called for making the police force of the country 'SMART' police force which is **S**trict and **S**ensitive, **M**odern and **M**obile, **A**lert and **A**ccountable, **R**eliable and **R**esponsive; **T**echno-savvy and **T**rained.*
>
> *Addressing the 49th Annual Conference of Directors General of Police/Inspectors General of Police and head of all central police organisations in Guwahati, the Prime Minister called upon every police station to create their own website to upload every week a true positive story of good deeds done by the police to change public perception and build positive image of the police among the people.*
>
> *Accessed on 26 June 2019 from* The Hindu *dated 30 November 2014.*

civilized society. This is embodied in the semantics of the word 'smart' itself.

To give effect to this sense of smartness is no easy task. It entails an organization-wide culture of service to society in the face of obstacles and impediments. There is also a much bigger import, that of changing the public perception about police and policing in general. A police organization cannot be called smart until it realizes that it is the very last *intervener* in a civil society. When everything else fails, police have to step in. Let me elaborate. A person desists from committing a crime till internal control and social control are working. As soon as these mechanisms fail, his crimogenic impulse forces him to take the final step for committing the crime. Police steps in at this juncture. If the crime is *yet* to be committed, preventive action of police works. If crime is *already* committed, investigation is set in to motion culminating in prosecution. This restores the collective conscience of society damaged by the crime, and acts as a deterrent against future crimes. An example of drunken driving explains the scenario. A person does not normally drink and drive, since a variety of controls, both internal and external, are working on him. When these fail, he drinks and hits the road. Police step in to prosecute the delinquent and in this process prevent accident and loss of life. At the same time, fear of law is restored. Whether for small crimes or for major disturbances like riots as

IIIT-D, Delhi Police sign technological MoU

A memorandum of understanding (MOU) was signed on Monday 24 June 2019 between Indian Institute for Information Technology Delhi and Delhi Police for setting up of Centre for Technology in Policing (CTP) in the capital. The set up will help police in identifying appropriate technology for crime investigations, maintaining law and order, managing traffic and gathering intelligence.

witnessed several times in recent history, police are the instrument of last resort at the disposal of a civil society. Failure of police leads to major upheaval with far-reaching ramifications.

This realization of the crucial role of police as 'an instrument of the last resort' also underlines the necessity to act, regardless of the impediments. Police do not have the luxury of postponing or not taking effective action on the pretext of lack of resources or being overburdened or for any other reason. Factors like uncooperative public, unreasonable media, lax laws, slow judicial process, poor funding and overburdened staff are, undoubtedly, impediments which affect policing. But a police force can be 'smart' only if it works despite them. Of the above-mentioned impediments, police can only take care of the first one, namely, public cooperation, provided the efforts are strategically planned and executed in a sustained manner in order to win the citizens' trust and confidence.

Delhi Police was perhaps the first police force in the country to realize the importance of seeking public cooperation and inculcating awareness among the people of not only their rights, but also their responsibilities. Most importantly, it created awareness about the limitations of police and the constraints under which Delhi Police works. In that sense, this was a smart strategy which was adopted in Delhi Police in the late 1980s. Having just recovered from the ignominy of the tumultuous event of 1984 anti-Sikh riots and still grappling with terrorist violence in the aftermath of operation Blue Star, Delhi Police adopted a new motto 'With you, for you, always' and with it a new vision of citizen-friendly policing. The emphasis of the top leadership changed to more humane policing and an effort to reach out to the citizens. It was a smart move in the sense that it was based on the realization that whether for anti-terrorist measures or prevention of traditional crimes, police cannot act without the active cooperation of the people. Several schemes were launched to bridge the yawning gap between the police and the public. The police organization which was perceived to be opaque and hide-bound was thrown open to the public. Visits of school children and other groups to the police stations were organized. Lectures, competitions and other events were held to project a friendly face of the police. The institution of Special Police Officer (SPO) was energized. SPOs were actively involved in crime prevention as well as law and order duties.

Apart from one-off events like 'Open days' at police stations, quizzes and competitions for children were organized. Alcohol and drug de-addiction camps as well as other citizen-friendly events became permanent fixtures in Delhi Police's calendar. Prominent among these was the Police Week, which is now celebrated every year during February, the month when Delhi Police became a separate entity in 1953. In order to involve the rank and file, various measures were introduced to promote a sense of regimental pride among the Delhi policemen.

This was a watershed moment for Delhi Police. After the serious loss of face suffered in 1984 by the assassination of the then Prime Minister, Indira Gandhi, by her Delhi Police bodyguards and the riots which followed, the initiatives proved to be quite strategically timed. It was also a smart move for another reason. It coincided with the strengthening of the human rights movement in India making Delhi Police one of the early adherents. The use of third-degree method, used allegedly by police forces to extract confession and solve cases, became passé and no longer acceptable. Scientific methods of investigation had to be adopted.

The corporate philosophy of throwing open the organization to public scrutiny and a complete disdain of the aggressive tendencies of police were initially viewed with incredulity. It was viewed by the organization as a passing fancy of the leadership which is divorced from reality. It was argued that the people-friendly face would be exploited by criminals and anti-social elements to have a free run without any fear of police. Among other things, the detractors pointed out deficiencies in the criminal justice system which the police, they argued, had to bridge with brutal methods in order to keep law and order in control. This was a period of ideological churning.

There was so much organizational emphasis on these outreach programmes that slowly the rank and file realized that Delhi Police had indeed turned its back to the old ways of thinking and working. The narrative had changed irreversibly. Slowly the entire organization started appreciating the need to take the people along. The values of citizen-centricity for policing started percolating down in the organization.

But this was a watershed moment for another reason. The organisation became more people-oriented and its polices were increasingly formulated in term of what the people perceived to be their pressing issues rather than what the police thought so. This process is continuing to this day. Apart from explicit efforts to involve the people in day-to-day policing through community policing schemes, there were diverse initiatives to bridge the emotional as well as physical distance between the police and the citizens. New police stations were opened in hitherto un-serviced and neglected areas, most of which were inhabited by the underprivileged sections. More and more officers started devising creative projects which brought the people closer to the police, like working with NGOs in slums, devising citizen-feedback system, and organising visits of police officers to residential colonies and educational institutions. With the advent of IT, social media and internet are being widely used for public outreach. Public grievance redressal mechanisms have been strengthened. The use of unlawful methods is not only frowned upon but severely punished.

One could see, even in the late 1980s, the seeds of *smart policing* although, the idea as used in modern parlance in the context of smart phones, smart cities and smart cards had not even germinated. The use of technology, citizen centricity, scientific investigation, human rights, behavioral issues, accountability and openness became themes for new policy direction. The foundation for smart policing had, undoubtedly, been laid. There was a lot of derision and sneers even among the public. They said instead of effective policing, Delhi Police is now indulging in drama. Its new motto 'With you, for you, always' became the butt of jokes. The media never shied from taking a potshot. Embarrassing captions, awkward photos or news items lampooning Delhi Police for any awkward moments and failings became a favourite activity. But it goes to the credit of Delhi Police leadership that not once did they lose nerve and roll back the people-friendly initiatives. Rather, a culture of introspection and self-improvement was encouraged.

THE WAY FORWARD

Over the years, changes have undoubtedly taken place in both the structure and culture of Delhi Police. But can we call it a smart police force in the contemporary sense? In my view it is still *work in progress*. There is a definite step towards making the force accountable, responsive and open in its dealing with the citizens.

Being a large force with law enforcement responsibilities spread over several terrains, it will be hard to pinpoint only few areas necessary for change. However, any discussion of smart policing would be incomplete without such an attempt. Therefore, I shall list possible areas, which are important from the standpoint of contemporary challenges. These areas require new ways of looking at law enforcement and adoption of innovative solutions as a response to these challenges:

1.**Crime reporting**: Police needs to record correctly and without bias any incident reported to it or which comes to its notice. Suppressing crime figures to show less crime becomes counter-productive as it leads to an increase in crime. There should be no attempt at statistical manipulation of any sort and the top leadership both at the organizational and political levels should discourage this practice. A true crime picture would result in less crime in the long run by keeping criminals on the police radar.

2. **Investigation**: Although there is increased reliance on scientific investigation, the process needs to be strengthened further by intensive training of Investigation Officers and by close supervision of investigation by seniors. Training facilities and labs for different areas of forensics need to be provided. Scientific methods are needed both for identifying the criminals and for prosecuting the cases in court in order to increase the conviction rate. This is also the best way to reduce complaints against the police for resorting to torture as a method of solving crimes.

3. **Crowd management**: In a democratic and populous country as ours, we have to deal with crowds on a daily basis. When crowds are friendly, as in a sporting event, police have to ensure only their orderly congregation and dispersal. But when they are confrontational, as sometimes they are, police being

the symbol of state authority, have to intervene to keep the peace. Police invariably become the target of their ire, even if the core issue has nothing to do with policing. Management of crowd is one area which needs strategic direction. There should be increased reliance on scientific tools for recording the activities of the crowd through CCTV system. A modern CCTV system should also be Artificial Intelligence (AI) driven, which can spot potential trouble makers and predict any untoward event. Social media analytics should also be widely used. In case of trouble breaking out, technology can be used to apprehend and charge the culprits. There are also modern systems of using force, like water cannons, taser bullets, etc., which are less lethal and, therefore, more acceptable. More importantly, imaginative solutions are needed by police officers to handle crowds, one of the major areas of public criticism.

4. **Traffic management**: The management of traffic in burgeoning cities like Delhi remains a big challenge. Even though we have good roads and modern vehicles, traffic congestion plays spoilsport and takes away the sheen from cities aspiring to be smart. Accidents are also a serious issue making it one of the most unsafe cities in the world. In the year 2019, 5,152 persons were injured and 1,463 persons were killed on Delhi roads. Police need to embrace technology in a big way to solve these traffic problems. There are technological solutions available for traffic regulations like the Area Traffic Management Systems (ATMS). For traffic law enforcement, there are solutions like CCTV cameras, Red light violation cameras and Speed cameras which record violations automatically. There is a need to have as little manual intervention as possible, whether in traffic regulation or traffic law enforcement. Delhi Police needs to make the road users of the city start obeying traffic rules and at the same time, slowly

usher in a modern traffic culture by spreading awareness and hand-holding the drivers to get used to modern driving habits like lane-driving, adhering to principles of *right of way* and respect for the rights of the pedestrians.

5. **Prevention of crime**: This being the very spine of police organization, Delhi Police needs to employ innovative methods to patrol the beats, gather grassroots intelligence and increase visibility. There is a need to involve the public and incorporate elements of both the old system of beat policing and modern methods of criminal surveillance.

6. **Intelligence**: Howsoever important it is for law enforcement, it remains an Achilles' heel for police organization. Police should overhaul their intelligence set up for effective collection, collation and sharing of actionable inputs for crime prevention, detection and management of law and order. Social media and other intelligence gathering and sharing tools need to be employed effectively with the support of top leadership in police.

7. **Training**: A very neglected area, police need to have an effective system for basic, promotion and refresher training in order to keep the police force up-to-date and relevant. More than anything else, effective training would improve police competencies in the long run.

8. **Collaborative policing**: To avoid various police units acting in silos, it is important that there is a culture of sharing in the organization. The units need to collaborate in law enforcement, sharing information, inputs and strategies for combating different types of crimes.

9. **Attitudinal changes and Soft skills**: Attitude of the entire police organization should bc changed to bring the needs of the citizens to the centre of all policing activity. There is a need to come out of the colonial mindset of police being the

instrument of power. Rather it should be seen as an instrument of socio-economic change. Since development process requires a peaceful law and order situation in the country, Delhi Police being the premier police force in the country should be the first to make this a vision statement for the force. Delhi Police should lead the way in inculcating the values of sensitivity to the citizens' needs. Police personnel require acquisition of soft skills like proficiency in English and Indian languages, effective conflict management skills, good communication techniques, computer and driving skills, inter-cultural sensitivity, gender sensitivity, and so on.

10. **Effective technology policy**: Delhi Police needs to strategically adopt state-of-the-art technology. If there is a delay, criminals would be one up on them. Apart from having an effective technology policy, there should be proper ownership of technological projects. In the coming years with rapid changes in technology, more and more projects are expected to be commissioned by Delhi Police. Many of these projects are of use to different units and districts. In such a scenario, one unit of police has to take ownership of the project so as to ensure proper handling, maintenance and periodic up-gradation. These projects should not become one-off events but rather should serve as the base for further advancement.

11. **Evidence-based policing strategy**: Delhi Police should adopt an *evidence-based strategy* for sharpening its response to law enforcement problems. Any police action or tactics like beat policing, mobile patrolling, neighborhood watch or even police *naka* or check-points should be evaluated on the basis of evidence so that it is targeted at the law enforcement problems effectively; its efficacy tested periodically and if needed, a course-correction undertaken. The three ingredients of an evidence-based strategy, viz.

targeting, testing and tracking, would sharpen the policing efforts and make it more goal oriented and efficient in the achievement of stated outcomes of policing, whether it is crime control, reducing harm or improving people's perception of police.

More than the list of what needs to be done, we also must look at the negative list of things a law enforcement organization of the importance and size of Delhi police should guard itself against. It is natural for any organization to become complacent. When such an attitude becomes dominant the organization stops growing. Delhi Police cannot afford to do that as the expectations of the people and the challenges it faces, are increasing by the day. It should be remembered that India has a young and restive population. They expect changes in the world around them and are impatient. They do not tolerate tardiness on the part of government agencies and the arrogance of authority. The *chalta hai* ('everything goes') attitude is no longer a viable option for any organization and particularly the police. We cannot remain impervious to change. In the present age, people want all information on their finger tips and all services delivered at their doorstep. Delhi Police cannot push the clock back. It cannot afford to postpone a serious look at its systems and processes in order to streamline the delivery of service to citizens in a transparent manner. Insensitivity to the needs of the public is no longer acceptable. Delhi Police does not have the luxury of refusing to deliver, citing organizational problems like lack of funds or shortage of manpower. It has to go around the impediments and deliver.

There cannot be wastage of resources. Internal administration of the police needs to be overhauled for this. We cannot have two persons doing a job which can be done by one. Wastage of manpower has to be avoided by the right human resource management (HRM) policy. Right persons are to be deployed for the right job and in right numbers. Some cost benefit analysis needs to be undertaken for all resources.

Similarly, we cannot afford to invent and reinvent the wheel. The knowledge which is a result of decades of invaluable experience and remains locked up in the organizational vaults need to be unlocked and used. The internal processes have to ensure proper management of the accumulated knowledge. Technology and modern management principles have to be used for effective dissemination of information. The top leadership should ensure that that all resources including information are optimally utilized for achieving organizational objectives.

Lastly, and most importantly, stress in the organization must be avoided. The work of police is inherently stressful. But the stress level should not be magnified further by the internal working of the organization. The onus, therefore, lies with those at the top leadership to promote a stress-free culture. The role of the SHO in this process is invaluable. Attitudinal changes through training and regular interaction and counseling of the staff have to be given high priority. It is also important to modify the ways of working in the organisation to avoid unnecessary stress for the cutting-edge levels.

Despite the many flaws it suffers from, Delhi Police remains the premier police force in the country. It is therefore incumbent upon it to score higher than any other police force, in being sensitive to citizens' problems and in its commitment to constant improvement. An important prerequisite is the well-being and welfare of its own men. The top leadership and all ranks should be conscious of the historical role of Delhi Police. All should strive to continuously raise their bar so that it becomes a role-model for other police forces not only in India but elsewhere too.

CHAPTER 13

The Daily Grind

Delhi Police in Action

So far readers have had a glimpse of the different units or branches of Delhi Police – both in terms of their individual structures and their processes. To complete the picture, they should be aware of how Delhi Police undertakes various tasks, which are of interest to the citizens. This is important because the tasks get accomplished not only by the functioning of the individual units or components but also their synergies with each other. The outcome is also conditioned by the ground realities, which keep changing over time and space.

At the end of the day, people may be more concerned with issues which they face in their daily lives–whether they are safe walking back home, whether their house is safe when they go on a vacation and whether they can enjoy mental peace when they sleep at night?

We have selected three areas to demonstrate Delhi Police in action – how the various components act and interact in order to achieve a strategic task at hand. These are control of Street Crime, Night Policing and Law & Order management. The intelligent readers will then be in a position to understand and appreciate the work of police in its context. They can underline the shortcomings in the policing strategy. Furthermore, police can gain tremendously from citizens' informed inputs, as they are the most important stakeholder, being both the recipients and the payers of police service. If the citizens are aware of the powers, capabilities and limitations of their police, they become active participants in the various law enforcement policies affecting their lives and their communities in a more meaningful way.

STREET CRIME

Control of street-crime is an area which is of great concern to citizens. Although, there is no explicit category as 'street crime' in criminal statues, the expression refers to crimes which take place in the open and includes robbery, theft and snatching. While theft and robbery are clearly defined in the Indian Penal Code (IPC), 'snatching' is a composite crime comprising two types of criminal action – use of criminal force and theft. An example is chain snatching, when criminal force is applied to pull a gold chain from someone's neck without his or her consent. Theft becomes 'robbery' when the victim is physically harmed or put under fear or restraint in order to commit the crime. For example, a criminal is said to have committed robbery if he puts the victim under fear of injury or death by pointing a weapon and orders him to part with some valuable property. If there are more than five robbers, the severity and punishment of the crime increase, and the crime becomes a dacoity. On the other hand, if a person's pocket is picked, it is simply a case of theft. Of the three types of crimes, dacoity is considered the most heinous followed by robbery, snatching and theft.

Delhi Police and other police forces in India consider street crime as a serious challenge. For me, it is also a touchstone of police effectiveness – in both controlling and solving crimes. I will explain how. The two main functions of police are prevention and detection of crime. For prevention, the main focus is on patrolling – whether on cars, motorcycles or on foot. Then there are other techniques like vehicle checking as well as stopping and frisking of persons at various checkpoints. All of these are performed on the street. Therefore, if criminals manage to commit crimes on the street, it is literally under the nose of the police. It is like they throw down a gauntlet at the police and their crime prevention strategy. The other part of the law enforcement action is detection of crime. Street crime again pose a challenge to police as the criminals spend at least some time in the street after the crime, trying to get away. It is a test of police effectiveness to stop and apprehend them before they succeed in escaping. And if they manage to get away, police has to unravel the clues left behind and solve the crime.

How does police tackle this bold and blatant professional challenge? When a call is received about a street crime, which may be from a victim himself, through the ubiquitous dial 100 facility of the PCR (now ERSS-112), an officer is dispatched from the police station. Meanwhile, the PCR van which is expected to reach the spot immediately, being the first responder, broadcasts some basic information about the crime and the particulars of the criminals. This information is relayed to all other PCR vans in the city, police check-points as well as other law enforcement assets like foot and motorcycle patrols. Sometimes, if the victim has been calm enough to note any distinctive feature of the criminals or their vehicle, these are also broadcast on the wireless network. Based on this description, there can be a fortuitous catch by an alert police officer somewhere in the city. But what if the criminals manage to get away?

A Delhi policeman knows that the information of a street crime is transmitted up the hierarchy and there is an immense pressure to work-out the case. 'Working-out' means arrest of the criminals and recovery of the stolen property –be it a motor vehicle, gold chain, cash or any other movable property.

Meanwhile, the officer from the PS upon reaching the scene of crime begins his enquiry. He also shares any specific information, which the PCR staff may have failed to note. He also takes down the complaint of the victim, noting down the minute details of the crime, for example, the colour of the vehicle, any weapon brandished by the criminals, the appearances and clothing of the criminals, his manner of speaking, any distinctive feature of his body and other details which might lead to his identification.

Back at the station, the IO completes the necessary paperwork, which includes registration of FIR. Meanwhile, his assistant, seeks to get the footage of any CCTV camera, which may have captured the crime or the movement of the criminals. Often the footage of several cameras have to be collected so as to trace their movement before and after the crime. This gives an indication of the directions from where they came and to which they escaped after committing the crime.

The Delhi Police have been collecting criminal data for many years now. These are stored in what is known as the "Criminal Dossier". This is an online database of arrested criminals and it is catalogued on the criminal's personal particulars, types of crimes, modus-operandi (MO) and other details. The victim of a crime is shown dossiers of criminals after short-listing the names from a huge database in terms of types of crimes, MO etc. If the criminal is not a first time 'novice' his dossier is likely to be available.

The effort of the police is to enable the crime victim to put his finger on some recognizable face, whether through CCTV images or through the criminal database. If he is not able to do so, which is quite possible if the criminal's record does not exist, either because he is a first timer or has never been caught, the police has to look elsewhere. One mechanism is to mobilize the network of secret informers. Crime investigators have a network of informers who have an ear for crimes committed in the locality. These are petty criminals who have links in the underworld and assist the police in investigation. Sometimes, they do offer useful tips which lead the police to a criminal or to a gang. The system of 'informers' is not institutionally sanctioned. It is very officer-oriented and some officers are more adept than others in identifying and engaging informers. But it is not necessary that only a police informer gives the tip. It can be an anonymous phone call or a common citizen who may tip off leading to detection of the crime.

Once the police are able to identify and short-list some suspects, the next and the most important part of investigation begins. Through the process of interrogation, the suspect is connected to the crime. More specifically, the suspect is put through a rigorous session of interrogation, by one or more officers. If they are able to do it well, develop an element of trust and make him 'talk', their first effort is to know the sequence of the crime – how it was committed, which vehicle was used, who were the associates and what happened to the stolen/robbed property. It is also possible that during the interrogation the suspect turns out to be innocent and is not aware of the crime.

Here, I shall point out that if a criminal confesses his crime in front of the police, it has no legal value, unless the admission of guilt is accompanied by the recovery of some material fact – for example, any weapon of offence or any property involved in the crime. Therefore, the second most important part of interrogation is to get the recovery effected on the 'pointing out' of the suspect. If the police are able to recover either the stolen property or any weapon or any other article, which can include a document like ID card or ATM card, then the police can be satisfied with its work. In the case of murder, it can be the discovery of the dead body if it had been disposed of or hidden by the murderers after the crime. The 'recovery' also conclusively connects the crime to the criminal.

After this comes a thorough examination of the suspect to further ascertain any other important details like his education, socio-economic background, his family, his associates, his friends, his hideouts and any other information, which the interrogation may lead to. Many of the collected information may not be relevant to the present crime but it can enrich the quality of information stored in the dossier of the criminal. This would prove useful in future crimes.

Another important information is that of receiver of stolen property. Any criminal indulging in street crime has to dispose of the stolen property – whether it is jewellery, a mobile phone or a car. An essential part of interrogation is to find out about the 'receiver' of the stolen property, which can form a part of the criminal's dossier along with other details. So next time he commits a crime, and he is identified by the victim, a secret watch is kept at the receiver's place which can lead to his arrest.

One question which the reader may be curious to know is whether force or duress is used during interrogation. You may recall that Delhi Police have already disavowed the use of third-degree method which includes physical torture or mental coercion as a means of eliciting information from suspects. Any professional police officer knows that this method is not only unethical but risky too. If it is found out that such methods were employed, even if it has led to 'working-out' of the crime, the IO will not have any support of his colleagues or seniors. He can be held legally liable for this act. And there is a high likelihood of discovery as there are set systems and processes within and outside the department for monitoring such abuse of power. Moreover, the arrested offender also undergoes a medical test prior to his production before a magistrate's court. If he complains to the magistrate and signs of physical injury are found on his person, the investigating officer can be held responsible and the legal tables will turn on him. Therefore, a good investigator will try and extort information by a mix of intelligent questioning and by establishing a relationship of trust with the suspect.

There are other means of tracking/tracing a criminal. In an earlier chapter, a reference was made to 'Beat system' and the network of beat officers in each police station. One important function of the system is collection of local intelligence which proves very helpful in solving crime and apprehending criminals. The beat officers keep a watch over the potential and active criminals in their beats. Whenever there is an unexpected increase or flaunting of wealth by a known or budding criminal, an alert beat constable will be inquisitive to know more. They try to find out the source of the wealth. If they are not able to ascertain the reasons, they either deploy their sources or even confront the criminals directly. If the suspect spills the beans, the beat policeman brings it to the notice of their SHO who will then pass it on to another police station where a property crime has been committed. This might actually lead to detection of the crime.

These days there is also a reliance on technology. For example, mobile phones, which are used extensively by criminals for communication, leave their own footprints which are be used by police to track and identify criminals. As mentioned earlier, there is a network of CCTV cameras in the city. These can be installed by government and municipal agencies or private persons for the safety of their own premises. These lead to detection of crime as the criminals leave a trail for the police to follow. It has also been seen that every crime committed with a peculiar modus operandi (MO) adds to the knowledge base of the police. They become wise, which helps to prevent such crimes and keep an eye on potential criminals.

There are very elaborate drills for prevention of street crimes. Every such crime is analysed down to the beat level. Questions are asked on all relevant tactical issues. How the incident took place, where were the police patrolling parties, were the PCR vans and the police checkpoints strategically placed to effectively deter criminals, and the like. If a criminal is finally arrested, a temporary break is put on such crimes as his associates try to evade arrest and therefore go underground. When the arrested criminals are released from jail, police keep an eye on such released criminals. If they indulge in crime again, their personal files are opened in which the activities of such criminals are recorded. If the criminals are incorrigible and continue to indulge in crime their 'History Sheets' are opened and their names are listed for surveillance. This gives the police an authority to monitor their movements and they can be called to the PS by the SHO for questioning.

Although, street crimes are an important category of crimes attracting a lot of police attention, there are other important crimes also for police – like crime against women and children, burglary, motor vehicle theft, kidnapping for ransom and extortion, not to mention heinous crimes like murder and riots. Sometimes, several teams are deployed to work out a sensational crime which may be attracting very adverse media attention or causing a public outcry.

Having detailed the process of preventing or detecting a street crime, I should add a caveat. The crime world is not static. Just as the police is upgrading its capabilities, so also are the criminals. They use technology, get specialized in different crimes, undergo training for various criminal activities and adopt various means to conceal their identity and movements. Sometimes despite very meticulous and laborious effort, a crime does not get solved. On the other hand, sometimes a difficult and blind case gets solved by very fortuitous turn of events. Elsewhere, a reference was made to the famous 'Tandoor Murder case' which got detected by night patrolling staff who noticed dense fumes emanating from the restaurant kitchen. They scaled the rear wall only to find the body of a woman being burnt in the oven of the kitchen. This coincidence of smoke and presence of inquisitive beat staff in the dead of the night led to the discovery and ultimately conviction of the murderers.

NIGHT POLICING

Now let us take another area of functioning to show how Delhi Police works. In the heading of the chapter on Police station, its round-the–clock functioning was highlighted. Readers may be wondering whether it is enough to ensure the safety of citizens at night just by keeping the station open round-the-clock. During the day, policemen and women, police vehicles and PCR vans are visible. Do they all retreat in the darkness? How is peace and tranquillity in the city ensured at night?

Having a system of policing during the night is vastly different than that during the day. During the day, visibility is important to ensure public order. But in the night, something more than mere visibility is necessary. During the daytime, it is neither feasible nor desirable to stop and question everyone on the road. Police can just keep a sharp eye on the movement during the day. But in the night, there are few persons on the road. People don't just loiter around. They come out only if there is a reason. For example, either they are returning home from night shift duty, a late-night movie or from a party. There are no shops, schools or offices open, so reasons for venturing out are few.

Therefore, a system of night policing must be planned keeping these realities in mind. Since fewer people are on the road, so fewer policemen are required. Their locations are also determined by the requirement of the area or locality. For example, in residential areas, the probability of crime is low as the residents are present inside. Only the houses which are locked, in the absence of the house-owners, are vulnerable to crimes like house-breaking and theft. But in market areas, all the shops are shut. Then, there are institutional buildings like offices and schools. All of these are vulnerable to night burglary. But many of these entities have their own system of night watchmen or private guards. These days there are CCTV cameras also installed. But still the work of police is cut out.

For one, they have to ensure that all the dark corners in the locality are well lit. The night watchmen deployed by a neighbourhood need to be kept alert so that they don't dose off in the dead of the night. Periodic inspections are made by the beat staff to ensure the CCTV and other citizen-installed security systems are functioning properly. After factoring in all of this, a system of night-checking is devised in order to enable them to check those out in the street so as to remove any doubt about their bonafide presence in the area.

Having explained the idea behind the night-time police presence, let me now explain how the night strategy of Delhi police looks like. Ever since the author started his career nearly three decades ago, the structure of night-time deployment has remained consistent. It is a legacy that has withstood the test of time. To understand how it looks like, the readers may recall that police force in Delhi is organized into 14 districts headed by a DCP, each district divided into 4-5 subdivisions headed by an ACP and each sub-division is divided into 3-4 Police Stations, each headed by an SHO. Going further down, each P.S. area has 3-4 divisions each of which is headed by an SI and there are 2-3 beats in each division. The night patrolling system is organized in a way that the area of responsibility of each rank is successively enlarged to the next higher rank's normal (daytime) area. For example, during the day 1 beat officer patrols the beat but in the night time with less people on the road, the night deployment is such that the area of patrolling of the beat constable increases to include all the 2-3 beats in the division. Similarly, the area of the SI extends to the whole of the P.S. and the area of the Inspector or the SHO to whole of the sub-division. By similar process of enlargement of the area, ACP looks after the whole district and there is one DCP in-charge of the whole city of Delhi. In order to make the system of night deployment robust there is a senior officer of the rank of Jt. CP or Addl. CP available on call, in case there is a serious crime or any law-and-order contingency requiring instant decision-making.

Apart from the deployment of staff, other sources like patrolling parties are also deployed in the PS area. Delhi Police has a fleet of motorcycles, which are also deployed for night patrolling. The PS night checking officer – generally of the rank of ASI & SI moves around on a motorcycle and keeps calling the patrolling staff on the wireless network –checking their physical presence and alertness. In addition, there are other vehicles in the area deployed on the orders of the district DCP. There are also special purpose mobile vehicles like Parakram/ Emergency Response Vehicles (ERV) etc, which patrol the area with specific roles like prevention of robbery/MV theft/terrorist attacks. These add to the police presence in the area.

In addition to the mobile and foot-patrolling resources, there are fixed police pickets in the area. These are meant to stop and check suspicious vehicles. These are either permanent (round-the-clock) pickets or night-time pickets. The pickets are selected very carefully, after analysing the pattern of crime and the topography of the area including the ingress to and egress from the area.

Having enumerated the network of night-time deployment comprising a synergistic network of foot patrol, vehicle patrol and pickets, the mode of policing also needs to be stated before closing. The night-time police presence can only be effective if anyone found in a public place at an unearthly hour is stopped and questioned. A family with small children cannot be expected to be out for some criminal activity. But if there is a group of able-bodied persons the likelihood of their being criminals is comparatively high. There is no ready-made solution. Police personnel have to use their common sense to discern who is suspicious and who is not. A good police officer needs to have the intuition and the sharp intellect to separate the bad guys from the good. The art of unobtrusive enquiry and subtle questioning can only come with training but above all, through experience of dealing with people. The more inquisitive a police officer is in knowing the truth, the better he gets with age.

At the police pickets also, the staff flags down a suspicious vehicle and questions the occupants. If need be, the boot of the vehicle is checked for any weapon, contraband or some stolen property. They may also ask for documents of the vehicle which could turn out to be stolen. The registration number can be verified from the database of stolen vehicles available with the police. Actually, the night staff manage to arrest a lot of criminals and seize stolen property every night.

The readers may be wondering that if the night policing system is so elaborate and fool proof why do crimes still take place. To this, one can only give the analogy of cricket. However well-placed the fielders are on a cricket field the batsmen would still make runs. However good the fielders are, catches would still be dropped. This is because there will always be blank spaces where balls can go, and the fielders can only chase. Similarly, police can never be omnipresent. The assignment of night staff is done keeping in view the availability of personnel, and there are always gaps in it. Lastly, it is my experience that however good your system of crime prevention and detection is, chance factors play a very important role in the arrest of criminals and working out of crimes.

LAW AND ORDER MANAGEMENT

The third area of functioning of Delhi Police, which I want to highlight is law and order. Law and order management can also be termed as crowd management. It goes without saying that this is one of the most contentious of all the domain areas of policing. And this is true of any police force in the world. Apart from crime, the biggest challenge to law enforcement and the establishment of order in society is by a hostile crowd, which may assemble for a specific purpose. If the crowd or public assembly is not managed well, public order is disturbed and there is a reasonable probability of break-down of law and order. Readers may be aware of the recent ransacking of the US Capitol by supporters of President Trump who had a free run inside a very protected place. Rightly, the Capitol Hill police was blamed for not being able to manage the protesting crowd.

But all public assemblies are not like that. For example, people congregating for a cricket match or a trade fair or a political/cultural meeting may be peaceful and may follow all the directions of the police. Other times, the crowds may congregate to protest against a government policy or a contentious issue. They generally display their numerical strength to prove a point. Then there are assemblies which may start off by being peaceful but turn violent as a result of some subsequent development, provocation or a mere rumour.

Crowd management is an important function of Police as gatherings have the potential of disrupting normal life. As against dealing with individuals, handling a crowd calls for a different skill set. Police have to ensure that the crowd assembles, holds the programme and disperses in an orderly manner without causing disruption to normal life. Ordinarily, there are two kinds of crowd management – scheduled or unscheduled. In scheduled, there is sufficient time available to the police before the actual crowd gathers. It is also generally peaceful. The agencies, inform and seek permission from the Police as per law. There is generally an 'Advance Liaison Meeting' held of all the stakeholders, which may comprise of the organizers, the venue owners, the event managers, the civil administration, law enforcement officers including traffic police and any other agency involved in organizing the event. Examples are arrangements for Republic day, Independence Day, India International Trade Fair, Auto Expo, any sports event like a cricket match or even a short duration event like a play or a dance recital which attracts a big crowd. Being the capital of India, Delhi also witnesses several political meetings and rallies each year. Sometimes, the crowd mobilization may be for an issue which may not be related to the city at all. But this is what democracy is all about. You have the right to assemble and express your right of free speech.

Then, there are the unscheduled or spontaneous public gatherings. These can happen as a result of sudden provocation or some incident without any prior notice to the police. A traffic accident, a crime like rape, or even a brawl can lead to sudden gathering. These can be peaceful or even turn violent. Setting fire to property, including public property, stone pelting, squatting on roads, blocking traffic, beating up passers-by are some of the manifestations of such violent congregations. These can be small in size or the crowd can swell to become large. Rumours and social media these days can transform a small localized issue to a large-scale conflict, engulfing the entire city or even the state in its fold. These are what are called riots. If they are between religious communities, they are called communal riots. The city has witnessed many such riots in the past. The NE riots at the end of February, 2020 was one such.

Needless to say, such spontaneous outbreaks of violence are a major challenge to Police. Police is trained in prevention and in investigation. But these fall in between. Prevention has failed and investigation cannot solve the emergent issue at hand. The mandate of the police in such a scenario is containment of the violence and to ensure that damage to humans and property is minimized.

It is not to say that police are caught totally unprepared and clueless in such a scenario. They have what is known as 'Riot schemes' which are contingency plans prepared by riot prone police stations and districts. These plans are standardized response framework which, have to be invoked after making adjustments for the specific context. I will explain how. The plan may prescribe use of force if the crowd starts indulging in violence. But what if the violence is caused by the relatives of a young child killed in a road accident and the crowd is not allowing the police to remove the dead body. Use of force by police here can lead to further escalation and also attract adverse community and media reaction. Police has no option but to remain patient and continue negotiating. There are certain attributes which help police in tackling such unforeseen situations. For me, it is how much the police in the area has maintained its contact with the population and how much it has developed close ties with the community with its work and conduct.

Police forces are very good at managing scheduled events. They do elaborate planning of the 'bandobast' or 'arrangement'. For this, a series of meetings are held. It starts with a request or application made by the organisers – detailing the programme, the crowds expected, the flow of events, any eminent artists, persons, VIPs invited, mode of invitation – whether through ticket, invitation cards, public notice, etc. All these are very important factors in planning the arrangement. After having a preliminary meeting with the organizers, the local police station plans out the arrangement. Views are also sought from other relevant units like Special Branch for some intelligence inputs, PCR regarding availability of PCR vans and 'outside' force to be made available and of course, traffic police for their own traffic management plan which forms a part of the main arrangement. A total synergy is ensured between the different branches of police – local police, PCR, traffic and any other like security unit which is responsible for security of any VIP visiting the event. If there are any outstanding issues, these are resolved by an internal meeting of the Police generally presided over by the senior most officer concerned with law and order, like a Joint CP of Range or the district DCP. After sorting out all the issues, the minutest details of the arrangement are worked out and a 'draft' arrangement is brought out. Then a final meeting is held at the proposed venue – the organizers and all the different stake holders as well as the police give the final shape to the arrangement. (The entire event flow is rehearsed to ensure that the arrival of the people, the staging of the event and the disposal is one integral process which takes place very smoothly and seamlessly. Traffic sub-plan which deals with the arrival, parking and dispersal of the vehicles is also tested to ensure safe and smooth traffic flow – dovetailing into the main event. All the while it is ensured that there is no serious dislocation in the law and order as well as the normal traffic system in the city).

After analysing the feedback from different agencies, changes in the overall plan of arrangement are made incorporating their inputs. A minute-to-minute programme is prepared so that all the players work on the same time-scale. After this is done, depending upon the size and importance of the arrangement a full-dress rehearsal is conducted, so as to acquaint every agency and the individuals of their role. Contingency plans are also formulated, and drills are carried out.

It goes without saying that the above steps are carried out very elaborately for massive arrangements like Independence Day and Republic Day. For others like a public meeting, a cultural programme or a cricket match these may not be as elaborate, but the idea of conducting a detailed planning exercise remains so as to ensure that there is no law and order breakdown.

Having said that, it is pertinent to point out that crowd management remains the biggest challenge for police. The unplanned and sudden demonstration or the accumulation of a crowd which starts indulging in violence does pose a serious challenge to policing. In handling such gatherings, the police feel hamstrung – if they do not take timely and effective action, the crowd may indulge in violence and arson destroying property and causing injury to people. They face criticism for such inaction, and rightly so. But if they take action and use force where members of the unlawful assembly are injured, police face criticism of being ruthless and insensitive. “Police lathi-charge peaceful farmers”, “Police beat up college students demanding bus service,” “Police show their brutal face against women protesting lack of drinking water”, etc. are possible headlines which may scream out the next morning. Police attract a lot of flak and have to do a lot of explaining for weeks to come. Often the higher judiciary takes cognizance and orders an enquiry. Each and every action of the police in handling the demonstration/ strike is minutely scrutinized and any wrongdoing is punished. It is not that such scrutiny should not be done. Actually, it leads to a lot of self-introspection, self-examination and course-correction within the force. It adds to the body of invaluable experience which does bring about improvement in the future. The only point here is that sometimes the gravity of the law-and-order situation can only be witnessed in real time. After a few days and weeks, it can no longer be felt. To judge any police action taken at the heat of the moment as an over-reaction may not be fair. In any case, the action of police should be judged in its context and not with a pre-conceived notion that police officers are trigger-happy. In fact, policemen and women are also a part of society and they don’t have anything personal against members of an unlawful assembly. They are just carrying out their duties, as mandated by law. It is natural that sometimes the quantum of force used may not be commensurate to what was necessary causing injury to some agitationists. What is ‘commensurate’ and what is not, is very contextual and difficult to assess objectively. A suggested approach is to apply the ‘counterfactual test’ by asking what would have happened if the police had not taken the action. May be this approach can help us assess the propriety of the police action.

The number of law-and-order arrangements the Delhi Police handle every year is phenomenal. These range from small gathering of protesters for something like a slum demolition or people demanding civic amenities to large ones like student or labour strikes. Most of these are handled with a lot of tact and patience. The rest of the city is not even aware of such happenings. Allegations of overuse of force, are few and far between. Every Police officer in Delhi knows that the right to assemble peacefully and to protest are the inalienable and sacred rights of every citizen in our country. As long as the protesters remain non-violent and do not disrupt ordinary life, police should remain neutral and cooperate with citizens. Only once in a while, when the crowd decides to go on the rampage that police intercede to restore order. On such occasions, police have to walk the proverbial razor's edge, between inaction and over-reaction, either of which may attract adverse attention from the community or media. A Delhi policeman or woman knows that we may survive this to fight another day.

Epilogue

Let me begin with a disclaimer. The idea of this book was only to demystify the Delhi Police and contextualize its performance for a proper and unbiased evaluation. It was not meant to be an apology for its past misdeeds and shortcomings. If at any point in the book such an intention is palpable, it may be attributed to limitations of the author's expression rather than anything else.

The description of Delhi Police covers only those aspects that concern the citizens, whether as recipients of its service or as members of the civil society with a stake in the health of an important organ of the state. These are also of concern to the members of the fourth estate to enable an informed reporting and, better still, an intelligent debate. These would also allow it to close the credibility gap between itself and the fast emerging social media, so that the latter becomes a complement rather than its competitor. Keeping this in mind, other aspects of police functioning like various administrative units and policies have not been dealt with. Some of these, for example, policies of procurement, finance, media management and HR are not directly of concern to the citizens. Only those aspects which have a public interface are covered. Those not covered, in any case, are already in the public domain or can be unravelled through the RTI route.

Delhi Police, in both its medieval and modern avatars, has seen and lived through the vicissitudes of the city's fortunes. It helplessly watched the massacre of Delhi by Nadir Shah and the plunder of its riches by several other invaders. It witnessed, first with hope, then despair, the 1857 mutiny, considered to be the First War of Indian Independence. It had a ring-side view of the bloody wars of succession in medieval India and the peaceful transitions of power in democratic India. It has been the cheerful harbinger of the Delhi Durbar in Imperial India and the first unfurling of the Tricolour in Independent India. It has enthusiastically facilitated the staging of prestigious events like the Asian Games, Commonwealth Games, NAM and CHOGM. It was badly bruised by unfortunate events like the Emergency and the anti-Sikh riots. And, it has been irreparably singed by the assassination of a prime minister by someone from its own ranks.

Through the ages, in happy and sad moments, Delhi Police has stood watch over the city. It has never rested and never stopped, aware of the reality that the good deeds may be forgotten but the bad deeds would keep reverberating in the collective psyche of the city. It is also aware of the constant scrutiny by the media including social media—both national and international, the judiciary—from the lowest to the highest and the legislature—from municipal to the national. No other police force in India is subject to such a critical and relentless oversight of its functioning. It still marches on, relearning, reengineering and reinventing itself. However much Delhi Police is vilified and mocked, it remains a role model for other police forces in the country. Even a small change introduced by it is minutely studied and emulated by others. This is the unique status of Delhi Police in the annals of police forces of the nation.

The journey of Delhi Police with its inseparable companion—the citizen of Delhi—however difficult it may seem at times, is not over yet. Many future generations of police officers would occupy the barracks and patrol the streets, each armed with a new skill-set and a mindset different from the one before. Nevertheless, there always would be the overriding aim of being sensitive to the needs of the people and a commitment to the goal of nation building. A time would come, it is hoped, sooner rather than later, that the elusive fit between the citizen's expectations and police performance is achieved. And, when that day dawns, books of this kind will become redundant.

Postscript

One cannot complete this book without a reference to the year 2020. It has been an unusual year. The incessant march of time will soon bury the year in the womb of history. But generations will continue to talk about it. Whether they would bestow it with adjectives like 'terrible' or 'transformative', only time will tell. However, it will not be able to ignore the fact that both individuals and institutions were affected and perhaps changed forever. Delhi Police, has also been transformed belying the expectation of people who hardly believed that a hide-bound immutable entity like it, could ever change.

For a police force which works amongst the milling crowds and has learnt to find a needle in the proverbial haystack, the sight of desolate streets was strange and at times jarring. Factories, mandis, shopping complexes were shutdown. Schools, playgrounds and residential colonies wore a deserted look. While patrolling the walled city you could hear your footsteps on the cobbled by-lanes. It was unprecedented the way the whole city just snuggled inside.

But very soon Delhi Police had to contend with a class of people they were familiar with but never had to worry about. The migrant labourers are the vast majority of people living in the shadows. They populate the back-lanes of posh colonies, the slums and the unauthorised settlements dotting the city. Their faceless presence keeps the rich households and the wheels of industry and transport moving noiselessly. The sudden lockdown left them without jobs and the only ostensible reason to stay back in the city. Coupled with the uncertainty of the lockdown's duration and the fear of the pandemic, the migrants decided to head home. To confine indoors, a determined multitude prepared to even walk hundreds and thousands of miles, in the absence of any transport, was no mean task. In the raging pandemic, the migrant labourers were endangering not only their own lives but others who were coming in contact with them."It is better to die in our janmabhoomi (birth-place) than our karmabhoomi (place of work)," the police had to hear this again and again.

It has been seen in numerous occasions that whenever the chips are down, Delhi Police works tirelessly and on several fronts. The resources with the police are limited. But, in collaboration with civil society, NGOs, and government agencies, they tried their best to ameliorate the conditions causing the flight of migrants from the city. An awareness campaign was started to advise the migrants to stay put till transport arrangements were made for them. Those who had vacated their rental accommodation were settled in make-shift shelter homes. Food and other essentials were arranged right at the people's doorsteps. All the police units chipped in, sometimes working for 12 to 14 hours at a stretch, meeting the migrants, cajoling them, convincing them and trying to make their plight tolerable.

Apart from these activities, the police had to enforce the lock-down and prevent the spread of the deadly disease. They had to work inside the infection hotspots (designated as containment zones) in order to make sure that essential services were available to the beleaguered populace. They were deployed in hospitals for providing security to medical staff from aggressive patients and their relatives whose numbers were increasing by the day. In the initial days, even essential equipment such as PPEs, masks and gloves were not available. There are heart-rending tales of staff not being able to attend to the urgent medical needs of their families, some with serious consequences.

It was not that the regular police work had completely stopped. Although crime rates had dropped but still, whenever a case or complaint was received, the police had to follow up as required by law. They still had to make arrests, search premises, attend courts (which later became virtual), take the injured to the hospital, and perform patrolling and picket checking duties. All these exposed the personnel to the virus. Delhi Police personnel staked their personal safety for the sake of society which needed a supporting hand. Needless to say, the department took a serious hit due to the disease. Nearly 7,600 staff members of all ranks were afflicted of which 33 lost their lives. The police leadership, at this juncture, took some very important decisions. They brought out a Standard Operating Procedure (SOP) for working at the time of the pandemic. It introduced many changes in the way we function, ensuring that the contact of the back-office staff with the high-risk categories was minimized and to avoid any unnecessary contact with the outside world. All the personnel had to strictly adhere to the SOP which included compulsory wearing of protective gear and social distancing in their day-to-day dealings. Personnel who were still getting infected despite the measures were quarantined at different locations earmarked for this purpose by the Delhi Police.

On the other hand, the pandemic offered enormous opportunities to transform the work culture in police. The department has given a digital push promoting the use of IT wherever possible. All the FIRs and complaints started getting registered online. Several online platforms and applications were initiated like Interoperable Criminal Justice System (ICJS), Complaint Monitoring & Tracking System (CMTS), Delhi Police Diary Management System (DPDMS), eBeat Book etc. which allowed seamless transfer of data and online processing and decision-making, greatly empowering the field staff. All meetings, unless face-to-face interaction was absolutely necessary, began to be held virtually over video link. Video is also used to speak to complainants, staff and other stakeholders. Even examination or interview of suspects are being done on video. The use of video technology not only minimised exposure to the corona virus but also saved precious time and energy.

But it was not just the pandemic which occupied the mind-space of Delhi police in 2020. Since the beginning of the year, tension was simmering in two of the biggest universities in Delhi. Jawaharlal Nehru University (JNU) was on the boil for issues related to the academic institution whereas Jamia Milia Islamia was agitating the newly enacted Citizenship Amendment Act (CAA) and the National Registry of Citizens (NRC). The students of JNU also came out in support of the latter on issues of CAA and NRC. The opposition to these issues was spreading to the wider population and in some areas, sit-ins were organised. People came and occupied some public places and roads as in Shahin Bagh in south-east Delhi. The Delhi Assembly elections were held amidst this charged atmosphere. The issue was fast turning communal in nature and before preventive steps could be taken, riots engulfed some areas of mixed population, especially in north-east Delhi. The riots took place when the US President Donald Trump was visiting India and the police had its hands full in making security arrangements for the high-risk dignitary. The riots were controlled after three days of blood-shed in which 53 lives were lost and more than 650 persons were injured. Delhi Police have a long experience of handling communally sensitive issues, but the rapidity and the intensity of the conflict this time round, took it by surprise. There are allegations and counter-allegations that the riot was an engineered one and timed to perfection. But all these are matters of investigation and would be unraveled subsequently.

In the closing weeks of the eventful year, farmer groups from Punjab and other North Indian states marched towards the capital. After having been stopped, they are now organising a protracted sit-in at several of the city's borders, protesting against the Union government's recently enacted Farm laws.

The pandemic brought into sharp focus the indispensable role of the migrants as also the immense philanthropic energy of the people of the city. This also gave a tremendous opportunity to Delhi Police to exhibit its public service capabilities which brought a lot of laurels to the force. It got the endearing tagline: '*Dil ki police, Dilli police*' implying that Delhi Police is close to people's heart. Moving forward, we need to ask how the positive image of Delhi police, earned during the pandemic, can be sustained over a longer period. In my view, it is capable of good work in normal times as much as in a crisis provided the good deed is not hidden by the wrong acts of a few of its personnel. Moreover, the police need to be unburdened by unnecessary chores which take away a lot of its time and energy. A lot of demands that are placed on the police can be handled by other societal institutions, existing or new. Matters like minor disputes in neighbourhood and in the family, filing false and motivated complaints against rivals, breach of contracts, removal of unauthorised encroachments, prevention of illegal constructions etc can be easily handled by other institutions like social welfare departments, family courts, municipal bodies and other dispute-resolution agencies. What is needed is a collective rethink of the role of the larger society vis-s-vis the police so that the latter can deliver their service better and in a more citizen-friendly manner.

As I finish writing the book, the scourge of 2020 is not over yet. In the month of January 2021 when the citizens of Delhi should be enjoying the balmy days of late winter they are still waiting for the loosening of the stranglehold of the deadly coronavirus which had tormented them for most part of the previous year. But being an optimist, I am confident that like so many challenges the city has faced in its history, this will also be forgotten and the city will move on.

***

Acknowledgements

Much of what I have written is courtesy what I learnt in my nearly three decades in Police. All positive or negative experiences I had as a cop have left a trail of wisdom which helped me grow both as an individual and as an officer. I am grateful to Delhi Police for giving me an opportunity to be a part of the force and for providing the wherewithal to look after my family. As a corollary, I am also greatly indebted to all my colleagues in the force, seniors and juniors, from whom I have gained invaluable experience in policing the capital city of India. I thank all Delhi Police Commissioners, past and present, who have steered the force through thick and thin and contributed in their own ways to make it what it is today.

I owe an enormous debt to my father who passed away when I was still in school but lived long enough to instill the values which have guided me since. My mother, who brought us up single handed against heavy odds, inculcated in me the strengths which she had in abundance and which I found very handy in coping with the tough and uncertain life of a Police officer. My wife Rakhee who married me while still in undergraduate college always kept pace with me in trying to share my burden of adjusting to our tough life. I can't recall a single occasion when she did not get up at dawn to prepare breakfast for an early morning *bandobast* or stay up late to open the door after my frequent late-night duties. The burden of bringing up two naughty children with little more than lip service from me, allowed me to concentrate my energies on my job. Being a good manager, she adroitly combined the smooth functioning of our household with a full time job to supplement my meagre salary. No word is big enough to thank you. I am also grateful to my two boys, Sidharth and Sarthak whose command over language and ideas I grudgingly concede as superior to mine. I consider them my friends, philosophers and guides. But much to my chagrin they often take this role too seriously and even pull me up in their different ways, for no other reason than to force me to shed my lethargy and raise my intellectual output. The book is in large part a result of their interpretation of our inter-generational friendship. I am greatly indebted to my elder siblings Dr. Swapna and Dr. Debashis and our not so big family which has always indulged me and showered me with a lot of love and affection.

I thank the talented but self-effacing Pushkar Thakur who not only designed the attractive cover but displayed immense patience in changing the various elements as many times as I asked. I am also thankful to our close family friend Madhu who willingly took up the boring task of editing my manuscript. Her effort made the work much more presentable than what it was before.

The valuable inputs provided by the ace editor and an old friend Sanjana Malhotra really enriched the quality of the book.

Lastly, I would like to thank my staff members Shankar Banerjee, Ved Malik, Arvind Kumar, Daljeet Singh whom we lost recently to Covid, Vijender Mohan and several others who with their efficiency and hard work kept my office functioning smoothly which enabled me to find time for the book. I lastly thank Pankaj, the silent efficient worker in my office who helped me prepare the manuscript and make it print worthy. I also sincerely thank all others, my close friends, understanding colleagues and the aware citizens of Delhi who touched my life in various ways and have made me what I am today.